The Coming Clash

THE COMING CLASH

The Impact of
Multinational Corporations
on National States

Hugh Stephenson

Saturday Review Press · New York

Contents

1

Sovereignty Undermined

On 5 December 1968, the *Wall Street Journal*, that internationally respected house organ of American business, carried the story of a rebellion. It was no customary act of American revolt, no student protest, no civil rights disorder.

It was a report from California that the wives of some executives were refusing to conduct their private lives wholly or even primarily in conformity with the wishes of their husbands' corporate employers. To a child of European liberalism, the shock of this report came, not from the rebellion itself, but from what it revealed about a society where such an event could be news.

That despatch from a reporter in Los Angeles was the starting point of this book. For, to an extent to which few of us are aware, the structure and quality of our lives is conditioned by the organisations within which we work. And the most important of these, in the non-Communist industrial world, are the great institutions of industry and commerce, the corporations, the banks, that dominate the "national" economies in which we live.

Further, the striking aspect of industrial development in the last quarter-century, above all in the last decade, has been the urgent drive by industry to expand beyond the bounds of any one country. The existence of international companies and banks is not new. But industry has been assuming an international basis at a rate and with an intensity that constitutes an entirely new phenomenon.

The creation or growth of today's industrial leviathans is the response to certain imperatives of modern technology and of the capitalist system as it is developing in the United States and

1

Europe. The trend is more evident and inevitable in some kinds of industrial activity than in others. This book is about these imperatives and these differences. But the focus is not on the technical and industrial factors behind the generation of these leviathans. It is on the implications and the consequences of their existence.

Above all, the focus is on the extent to which these modern corporations contradict traditional ideas about nation states. This contradiction goes far beyond immediate and narrow implications of national sovereignty, as these are usually construed by politicians and lawyers. It is not just, or even mainly, a question of whether international companies can circumvent particular regional laws and regulations. It is that our whole framework of thought and reaction is founded in the sixteenth-century concept of the sovereign nation state. Outside that framework, as individuals, we know no points of reference. We are refugees. For on that framework the whole substance of social and political history has been built for the better part of four hundred years. In narrow economic terms alone, the sovereign nation state remains the basis for our policies towards industry, towards taxation, towards industrial monopolies, towards trade through imports and exports, towards the whole trade-union movement.

In this sixteenth-century framework, the international corporation is an intruder. In response to the requirements of modern technology and large-scale industrial organisation there have developed some three to four hundred companies, the majority based in the United States, whose range of industrial activities overrides this national framework. These new leviathans, with an international existence of their own, dominate the commanding heights of modern industry, above all in the newest and fastest growing science-based industries. And national governments are having to adapt their fundamental attitudes and practices, or else risk the consequences of falling behind in this present phase of industrial evolution.

The lawyers, to be sure, will do their best to preserve the forms of national sovereignty. For the nature of law and political

2

theory is conservative and its practice is to defend a framework of theory even after reality has in fact changed. But in substance, rather than form, our political system is already adjusting to satisfy the requirements of these new corporations. The important issues are not legal and political. They are social in the widest sense. For these corporations have a style of action and a pattern of requirements that is new. They affect critically the lives of those who work for them and the societies in which they operate. More important, perhaps, they are changing the whole pattern of economic relations between one country and another. For these relations are based traditionally on the notion that the main economic and industrial contact between countries is through trade. We are invited to experience vicariously a sense of national pride when exports rise and dejection when they fail to do so. We give public honour to industrialists for their services to exports. We tailor our domestic economic policies, we devalue our currencies, in order to fulfil national targets for the balance of trade. Yet, more and more, international corporations are rendering this notion invalid.

Statistics, as for many other purposes, are here less than satisfactory. There is, in fact, no official figure for the value and growth of foreign investment by companies. The only figure that features in official estimates (American, British, or other) is for the "book value" of these investments, the value at which overseas investments still happen to be entered in company balance sheets.*

By the end of the 1960s, this "book value" of foreign investments by companies based in the United States, Europe and Japan was alone well over $100,000 million. The true value of such investments could have been anything up to twice that figure, or some $200,000 million worth of the physical assets – the factories, plant and machinery – that make up the fabric of national industries. On this evidence, the production by these foreign subsidiaries was by 1970 already greater than the total value of world trade. On top of that, the internal operations of international groups form an increasing part of what appears

* On this question of "book values" and company balance sheets, see page 22.

3

in the figures for world trade itself. In the case of a country like the United Kingdom this trade within companies themselves, for example with motor-car components made in one place for assembly elsewhere, probably accounts already for something over 25 per cent of all British imports and exports.

Foreign ownership of industry in Western countries has been growing more rapidly than any other aspect of their economies. During the 1960s, it grew at a rate of something like 10 per cent a year, or $2\frac{1}{2}$–3 times as fast as the average growth rate of the national economies themselves. Thus by the late 1960s, the direct activity of international companies had become the single most important link between industrial countries, though the notion that this was still trade continues to be the basis for national economic policy and thinking. It is increasingly important that national policies and attitudes should rapidly adjust to this new reality.

There is nothing directly new about individual citizens and companies of one country investing money in another. What is new is the volume of such investment; and its concentration in the direct control of manufacturing industry. And here the major change since the middle 1950s has been in the direction and character of American overseas investment. The proportion going to the rest of North and Latin America has dropped sharply. At the same time the proportion going to Europe and Japan has doubled. There has, equally, been a sharp concentration of investment in manufacturing industry, in place of the former heavy predominance in plantations, like those of the United Fruit Company in Latin America, and in mining.

In Europe's investment relations with the United States, there was persistently heavy investment on Wall Street in stocks and shares, but little direct investment until the 1950s. Before 1939 British investment in the Americas was largely of this portfolio kind, or in the form of loans to finance the building of railways, ports, or urban tramway systems in South America and elsewhere. One estimate is that British and other European investors already owned something like 5 per cent of all United States capital in this way by 1900.[1] But this kind of investment was and

4

is different from direct investment where the clear purpose is to affect or control the management of the subsidiary companies involved.*

In absolute terms, this development of international industry has been dominated by American corporations, for reasons which are examined later, and, to a lesser extent, by British-based companies. In the twenty-five years after 1945, United States based companies established more than 8,000 new subsidiaries in foreign countries. Something like 80 per cent of all investment in foreign countries by the end of the 1960s was owned by British and American parent companies. As a result of this trend, by the middle of the 1970s, it is likely that not much more than 10 per cent of American industry's total sales in the rest of the world will be directly exported from the United States. The other 90 per cent will be manufactured abroad by American-owned and -controlled subsidiaries. Production by these subsidiaries could thus be something like eight times as important as American industrial exports themselves.

In relative terms the process has already gone as far in other industrial countries like Britain, the Netherlands and Belgium. The Royal Dutch Shell group, with its Anglo-Dutch base, is as large as Esso. The Anglo-Dutch Unilever concern and British Petroleum each has a turnover more substantial than the budget of the Spanish or Australian government. The subsidiaries of British-based companies in other countries were, already by 1970, manufacturing twice as much as the whole of British domestic industry's direct exports. Even France, not a country that immediately springs to mind as the mother of international corporations, has subsidiaries in other countries which produce as much as the total of French exports. And Swiss-based companies have more investment in other countries in relation to the size of the Swiss population, than do American companies.

* Other pre-1914 investment by European countries was, for the most part, firmly within the colonial framework, though there was substantial French and Belgian money in pre-revolutionary Russia and German money in the Austro-Hungarian Empire.

Yet overall figures, even on the scale of those for international companies, rapidly lose meaning. Some examples might serve to put today's industrial and financial giants into perspective against the nation states across whose boundaries they operate.

Take International Business Machines (IBM). The research and development costs of the so-called third-generation IBM computers* was in the region of $4,500 million. This was something like double the money spent on the war-time Manhattan project to produce the atom bomb that was dropped on Hiroshima.

Or take General Motors. The turnover of General Motors, at some $24,000 million a year, is significantly greater than the value of the entire annual economic activity† of Belgium or Switzerland. Its annual world-wide wage and salary bill, at some $7,000 million, is roughly equal to the annual value of all economic activity in Greece. And, if the comparison is made with the annual budgets of the governments concerned, a more significant figure for economic and industrial decision-making, the discrepancy would be even more stark. From its sales outside the United States and Canada, General Motors earns an income of some $3,400 million a year, or roughly the equivalent of the Swiss national budget.

The comparisons could be continued endlessly. The point is simply that the general public in industrial countries, even perhaps those managers and executives directing their fortunes, have not yet grasped the full scope of the financial and industrial power of these institutions. The extent and character of their growing passed somehow with little notice in the twenty-odd years after 1945.

They are not all-powerful, any more than any government, even that of the United States or the Soviet Union, is all-powerful. The government of a weak Libya, with revolutionary aspirations, can and does win tactical battles with the giant oil companies, if it plays its cards with conviction and nerve as it

* Based on micro-circuits in place of the transistors in second generation computers.

† Taking the figure for gross national product.

6

did in 1970 and 1971. In just the same way, a revolutionary movement in Vietnam has withstood the military might of the United States in a guerilla war. There is also the view that impressive figures for global turnover or the value of physical assets exaggerate the importance of this growth. This view has been expressed, for example, by Maurice Zinkin, economic adviser to the giant Anglo-Dutch Unilever concern.

The Chairman of General Motors himself does not have the power of a local councillor who can compulsorily acquire our house, or of a bishop who can tell us not to family plan, or even of the star in the Michelin Guide which tells us where to eat and drink. As for the politicians who tell us what taxes we will pay, how much fruit there will be in our jam and what hours we may buy our drink – the mere comparison of a businessman with them is ridiculous.[2]

If Zinkin has a point here, it is that substantial aspects of everyday life are negligibly affected by the structure of industry, or for that matter by the decisions of government. For each of us in our everyday Western industrial lives there are many more important factors than whether this company or that is British- or American-owned, even where it is our own employer. But this is a view valid only for one particular and limited range of vision.

For there are substantial areas where the influence of government on everyday life is critical, where the institutions of modern industrial society affect, for good and for bad, the quality of life. To our medieval forebears famine, disease and the church were the omnipresent influences on life. Today, in industrial countries, our lives are dominated by the fact that we live as part of a "modern" industrial complex. The international corporations are playing a daily greater role in shaping this complex and thus in shaping our societies. The relative power and influence of these commercial and industrial agglomerations is greatly underestimated. For, whether consciously expressed or not, they have clear and inevitable social and political interests. They develop a self-generated impetus, quite different from the personal drive of traditional capitalism. And this materially affects the sort of society in which we live. Their interests increasingly conflict with

7

and disturb the comfortable conventions about the divine rights of the sovereign nation state to which post-Renaissance history has accustomed us in the West.

There is a school of opinion which holds that, since these international corporations belong to the sort of international growth to which we are committed, we have no option but to make our accommodation. It may be so. Yet it should still be worth the effort of asking two questions. First, what exactly has been the nature of this change towards international industry? What have been the practical consequences and what are the present trends? The second question is why. Why have there been these pressures on industry to break out of national bounds? And will they continue? This is the only basis from which to look at the consequences for our social and political systems.

It is no answer to stress that some industry has been international in some senses for decades, even centuries. For the degree and pace of this process in the past ten years have been a phenomenon without historical parallel. It is also of little point to indulge in a neo-nationalist reaction of the sort that produced the celebrated, though facile, outcry from Jean-Jacques Servan-Schreiber in 1967.[3] He saw the process exclusively as an American industrial invasion of Europe. His counter-measure was a Europe organised as a political unit to confront the challenge. The analysis suited a Europe accustomed to a decade of Gaullist oratory about the virtues and strengths of autarchy. Yet the analysis was false. And the trends of the late 1960s were proving it false at about the same time that his best-selling book was making its mark.

The picture that should have been painted was of American-based companies in the van of a movement which has taken whole sectors of industry down the path of international integration, a path mapped out in the period between the wars by the great American and European oil companies, including the Anglo-Dutch Royal Dutch Shell and the British Anglo-Iranian.*

* Originally Anglo-Persian and now British Petroleum.

It is a lead that European and, more slowly, Japanese industry has been following with growing energy in the interval. There are many reasons why American companies were at the front of this movement and they are examined later.* The central fact for the industrial countries of Europe is that it was and is a challenge of size and operational flexibility; not, by its nature, a peculiarly American challenge.

This is the central feature of this changed international pattern during the 1960s. Modern industry discovered the advantages of mobility from one country to another, from continent to continent, and proceeded to conduct itself accordingly without regard to national boundaries. Meanwhile politicians, economists, trade-union leaders and ordinary citizens continued to think and act as if industry were tied by geography. It seems, for some reason, as if the managements of some international companies alone have found a formula for removing themselves outside our framework of national states. Politicians, internationalists and others variously preach the need, or the inevitability, of positive supranational thought and action. Only some modern businessmen, within their sphere, have found a manner of achieving it.

This process has produced a growing list of companies where foreign investment and manufacturing are an equal or more important part of their total operations than their domestic activity. Taking the Americans first, Standard Oil of New Jersey (Esso), International Telephone and Telegraph (ITT), Singer, Colgate-Palmolive, Mobil Oil, National Cash Register (NCR), Corn Products, Goodyear, Sperry Rand are all giant corporations, which have approaching half (some of them over half) of their fixed assets outside the United States. There are scores of smaller corporations (small that is only in the American context) in the same position, like International Packers, Burroughs, H. J. Heinz, Charles Pfizer, Warner-Lambert Pharmaceutical, Gillette or Crown Cork and Seal. Foreign operations contribute anything between 30 and 50 per cent of the total profit earned by such giant American corporations as

* See pages 31–47.

9

Eastman Kodak, Caterpillar Tractor, International Harvester or Minnesota Mining and Manufacturing (MMM). IBM now does more than a third of its total business outside the United States.* ITT, with a much longer history of running international subsidiaries, had a payroll of 128,000, or 70 per cent of its total work force, in Europe by the mid 1960s. Some European companies have become even more international. The prime example is Nestlé, Switzerland's largest company and in many ways a very local concern,† which in fact does no less than 98 per cent of its business outside Switzerland. A substantial number of European manufacturing companies now get more than half their profits from foreign operations, for example the German chemical company, Bayer, or the Dutch Philips concern, or British Oxygen.

The fact that big business alone has discovered the institutional forms required to move freely without being tied by national boundaries has wrought a fundamental change in the balance of power between industry and government. This, simplified, is the whole issue of government regulation, or support, for industry; and the supervision of industrial activity to ensure socially acceptable behaviour, through policies designed to maintain or further encourage competition, high standards and low prices. The capacity of international industry physically to move its location, or the realisation that it could, has significantly altered its relationships with governments.

This footloose quality of manufacturing is now a real factor in the prosperity of industrial regions. Governments know that they cannot afford to ignore it. Within obvious limits, a corporation operating on an international scale has a flexibility

* With its dominant position in world markets well established, this is a highly profitable part of its total business. For, while foreign sales in 1969 represented 35 per cent of IBM's overall total, they contributed 43 per cent to the corporation's total profit figures. The scope of these IBM foreign operations is illustrated by the fact that this 35 per cent of total turnover was worth twice as much as the entire value of British exports of manufactured goods in 1969, a year when all previous British exporting records were soundly broken.

† Shareholding in Nestlé is exclusively in the hands of Swiss nationals or residents.

about where to put its new plants and which, if any, of its existing plants should be expanded or run down. This is a flexibility denied to more purely national concerns.

This changed balance of power, which requires governments to make tax concessions and pay money by other means to some of the world's richest companies, in order that they and their citizens should have the economic advantages that result, has been a permanent theme in the industrialisation of developing countries. The new element since 1945, and particularly through the 1960s, was the way in which this pattern also spread to the industrial countries themselves.

The consequence is that governments will have increasingly to harmonise their regulations and practices, if they are not continually to be drawn one by one into a Dutch auction. In part, individual governments have already lost their freedom of action. No industrial or developing country today can afford to introduce rules and regulations affecting industry and commerce, particularly in the area of taxation, which are significantly more stringent than the average. The freedom of government action in this respect has gone, because international industry can and will make dispositions to by-pass single countries or geographic areas, where its legitimate requirements are not largely met. The term of art widely used is that the "investment climate" must be attractive. It is employed most often by businessmen from industrial countries when considering the policies of developing countries. It indicates the lack of freedom left to governments in major social and political questions, if they wish to continue in the mainstream of industrial and economic development.

This argument has been put in its starkest form by Franz Ulrich, chief executive of West Germany's biggest commercial bank, the Deutsche Bank. Asked for his views on investment by international companies in developing countries, he answered,

A prime necessity, as I see it, is the improvement of the investment climate in the developing countries themselves, as well as an improvement in the whole attitude towards private property and in particular towards foreign business activity. . . . In the longer term the necessary

11

investment climate will be created by sheer force of circumstance, because automatically investment capital will flow to those countries providing the necessary conditions – and there are already a number of them. The others will undoubtedly learn the lesson and follow suit in their own interest. After all, if the countries now inviting investment capital were acting as investors themselves, they would insist on exactly the conditions we are asking for now.[4]

Ulrich was here speaking with less circumlocution than is usually employed on this delicate subject. But politicians in developing countries know the price in lost political and social freedom that they have to pay for economic progress.*

It has been the central dilemma of political economy for the developing countries. They may want the material benefits that come to them through the local subsidiaries of companies based in industrial countries; but at the same time they may wish to preserve or develop inconsistent social and political attitudes. It is, however, no longer a dilemma for developing countries alone. Governments and public opinion in the industrial countries, comfortably accustomed to think of their countries as bases for international companies operating abroad, will with increasing force come to realise that they are themselves hosts to just such companies. As this process develops, one would expect to see social and political reactions within industrial countries, similar to those which have been considered immature from politicians in the Third World during the 1960s.

It seems in fact, to use a symbolic form of expression, that there is no realistic middle position for the single nation state today between accepting the requirements of international industry and following the path of Castro's Cuba: accepting all the social and economic consequences that either course involves. For the government of a single nation state, operating by

* This was, for example, the express theme of one conference at Amsterdam in 1969, arranged by the United Nations, at which such a noted moderate amongst American businessmen as David Rockefeller, Chairman of the Chase Manhattan Bank, and such a noted moderate amongst African politicians as the late Tom Mboya, Kenya's Minister for Economic and Development Planning, were invited openly to explore together ways in which their interests could be reconciled.

itself and with responsibility for its own industrial and economic performance, there is no real middle ground between these two extremes. This contraction of choice for individual governments, as we know them today, is the unavoidable consequence of the way in which substantial sectors of modern industry increasingly operate. It is the reason for the rapidly growing irrelevance of the traditional socialist approach to the fundamental issues of political economy.

For, in the international industrial world that is growing about us, there is a dated unreality about the idea that the state can control the "commanding heights" of its own economy. It is equally dated to suppose that "national" industry can now be directed for "national" planning purposes. For large-scale modern industry, most especially at the high technology end of the spectrum, must increasingly be part of an interlinked and international network of production and sales. Otherwise it will not be commercially viable. The choice, within the present structure of nation states, is therefore limited. Either the political and social framework is adjusted to suit the requirements of large-scale industry, or a social and political experiment is conducted outside the mainstream of industrial advance. This is not a question of state ownership or part ownership or control. It has to do with the objective facts of modern technology. The oil industry is the prototype. For there is no such thing as a national oil industry. There are only a small number of large companies, based legally wherever they may be, engaged in finding and producing oil in one place, and transporting, refining and selling petroleum products in another.* In that industry there is little noticeable difference between the behaviour of Standard Oil of New Jersey, owned wholly by private shareholders; British Petroleum, almost half-owned by the British Government; Ente Nazionali Idrocarburi (ENI), or the Compagnie Française des Pétroles (CFP), which are wholly owned by the Italian and French Governments respectively.

---

* The only partial exception has been the United States which is at once a major oil producer and the major consumer of oil products.

The lesson, in fact, for nationalists and socialists alike should be that a single nation state, exercising its sovereign rights, now lacks the scope effectively to match that of truly international companies. If either group wishes, at a political and legal level, to exercise more control or supervision, then a correspondingly wider reaction is required. This is now, more than defence or traditional foreign policy, the strongest argument in favour of increased supranationalism at the political level.

In terms of the relationship between industry and politics, to use a phrase coined in another context, the medium is the message. The lesson that the oil companies demonstrated first and most conclusively is that, in an industry with heavy capital requirements and where the end product is without national characteristics, the only viable long-term strategy is one that ignores as far as possible the political and cultural divisions of the world into countries. For a barrel of crude oil is a barrel of crude oil, whether it is sold by Shell in the United States or Mobil in West Germany. The fact that oil and all the products that come from it are in this sense homogeneous, regardless of the market, is the reason why the oil industry is formed by companies operating on this international basis. There was no question for them of having to create markets for a "foreign" product in different countries.

The development since 1945 is that ever-growing sectors of industry are moving more or less rapidly into the same category as the oil companies. The style of marketing methods may still vary substantially from country to country. But nylon is nylon in Austria, Andorra or Australia. The product is the same and the method of production is wholly exportable. This applies to the entire range of man-made fibres, as it applies to the bulk of the modern chemical industry's output. It is no accident that the chemical companies became the second major wave of international enterprise: and with them companies in the related fields of pharmaceuticals, man-made textiles and synthetic rubber.*

* For example, based in the United States, Goodyear, United States Rubber, Firestone, Dow Chemicals, Du Pont, Esso, Mobil, Texaco, Gulf Oil, Standard

Increasingly over the past twenty years, this homogeneity has spread over the industrial spectrum. By the end of the 1960s, it had gone much of the way in the world motor-car industry. In the early days of motor cars, there was a significant difference between a British, French or German car. There is still a difference between the cars required for the bulk of the United States domestic market and those required in Europe; but within Europe there is an unmistakable trend towards interchangeable models. This at once allows the rationalisation of production, particularly in the making of components, on an international basis. Such by itself is the qualitative change in the European operations of, for example, General Motors, between 1930 and today.

Electronics and computing, the most rapidly expanding of all industries in the 1960s, were fields again where the basic product was identical for all markets. The companies involved in producing electronic data-processing equipment (and the sophisticated components for them) have grown with the industry itself in the post-war era. Thus it is the modern industrial sector that most clearly indicates the direction in which modern capital-intensive industry is moving.

The 1960s saw the reaction of industry to two further factors. The first was the explosion in research and development costs for many new industrial products. The second was the increasing availability of mass-production methods. Both factors constituted major pressures for the internationalisation of industry.

It is surprising that this process of adjustment was only gathering real pace as late as the 1960s. But historically, mass-production and billion-dollar technology are both essentially the products of the Second World War. Henry Ford pioneered production by assembly line between the wars at Dearborn, Michigan, but it was the demand of war-time production that

Oil of California; and others like the British companies BP, Dunlop, Courtaulds, ICI; or the Anglo-Dutch Royal Dutch Shell group; or the French Rhône-Poulenc, Michelin, Air Liquide, Roussel; or the Dutch AKZO; or the Swiss CIBA-Geigy, Sandoz, Hoffman-La Roche; or the Belgian Petrofina and Solvay; or the German Bayer, Hoechst and BASF; or the Italian Montecatini-Edison and Pirelli.

forced the motor-car and other industries to face up to these lessons of mass production. When, in 1936, Charlie Chaplin produced his film *Modern Times*, that great statement of the conflict between industrial mass production and individual liberty, it was an inspired piece of prophecy, not reportage.*

A standardised product, mass production or continuous-process manufacturing, and rapidly growing research and development (or exploration) costs: these are the primary features of the oil industry; the related chemical and petro-chemical industry; the manufacture of motor vehicles; of business machines – from typewriters and desk calculators upwards – but particularly of computers; of tyres, soaps and detergents, farm machinery and the whole range of electrical and electronic products. And such are precisely the industries into which foreign investment, by American companies in Europe and elsewhere, was concentrated between 1955 and 1970. With the exception of motor vehicles, these are also the categories in which foreign industrial investment in the United States is now concentrated. For identical reasons these are the industries in which there is a growing concentration of power in the hands of relatively few companies at the national level as well. In the single particular case of electronic computers, IBM is approaching the status of a world monopoly.

In these industries, the demands of international production come firmly into conflict with traditional policies, designed to promote healthy competition and avoid the consequences of monopolies. Indeed, the existence of dominant international groups in these industries has already made an anachronism of individual national policy towards monopolies, cartels and industrial competition in general. For these industries are increasingly structured on what economists call oligopolist lines; where a handful of corporations, usually with one or two in a leading position, have the power to set price levels for the market as a whole. Leaving aside the possibilities of collusive

* The theme was still sufficiently fresh for it to form the background of a British film in 1960, Karel Reisz's *Saturday Night and Sunday Morning*, starring Albert Finney.

agreements, in such a situation there can be no real competition of the sort that theoretical advocates of free-enterprise capitalism admire so fervently.

For the companies involved are primarily concerned with the status quo; with preserving their share of the market; with ensuring that the market remains orderly. The major oil companies operate in this way as an international oligopoly, largely outside the control of individual governments. The major airlines have operated on the same lines of co-operative price-fixing, though here it has been done overtly and with government backing through the machinery of the International Air Transport Association (IATA). The pattern is now spreading to other industrial sectors. In the motor-car industry, for example, the dominant influence on price levels throughout Europe is the structure set by General Motors. The major oil companies effectively charge the same price for their products and raise prices virtually in unison, even though there is no formal or informal price-fixing cartel in this instance. They do so because they are, within very broad limits, facing the same production costs; and because, with their anxiety to ensure steady, full use of their expensive refining and other plant, they are more interested in a stable market and in protecting their share of it than in any exceptional gain from the dangerous and speculative game of competition and price wars. Competition for market shares exists in such an "oligopoly" situation but it is emphatically not a competition based on competitive prices.

This development has substantial implication for the traditional pattern of economic policy at an international level. For the interests of the giant international corporations can and *do* conflict with the generally accepted trend since 1945 towards ever freer international trade, based on international agreement. And there are signs that governments *are*, in fact, adjusting their policies to the changing requirements of the corporations. It is likely that they will do so increasingly during the 1970s. In that event, we may look back on the period from 1945 to 1970 as the burgeoning of a then-blighted movement towards trade liberalisation; a movement born from the ashes of the damaging and self-defeating economic nationalism of the interwar period; a movement rendered irrelevant, because it did not fit the new character of international industry.

The central feature of this change is that such wide areas of critical decision on economic and industrial policy have become matters within the discretion of corporate managers. These include questions like the flow of imports and exports within a group or company, from one country to another. By extension, they include the distribution of employment between one country and another.

These are the sort of questions that have historically been the province of national governments. It is to this changed balance that governments and trade unions alike have so far entirely failed to adapt their basic attitudes and policies. During the 1960s an extravagant measure of attention was paid to the superficial manifestations of international industry. This, again, was largely because of the hypnotic influence that General de Gaulle and his particular notions of national sovereignty and independence exerted on the decade, even for those who disagreed with his singular vision. It was the reason for such concentration on essentially irrelevant issues, like the threat that international corporations might pose to national security. The real issue, however, goes to the heart of economic policy.*

American-based companies have been pace-setters in this development, which affects every aspect of the relationship between corporations and nation states, together with their citizens, be they thought of as managers, workers or consumers. It has therefore, until now, been mainly (almost exclusively) on American-based corporations that attention has been focused.† But there seems to be no evident reason why the performance and interests of American corporations should be significantly different from those of another home base that are now following in their wake.

* For a fuller discussion of the anti-free-trade influence of some international corporations, see pages 90–4.

† This is the reason why a number of American corporations, like IBM and General Motors, feature so much in the writings about international companies (and in this book).

18

Professor Pierre Uri, the French economist, referring in this context to the effects of American industry's transmigration in the last twenty-five years, has said: "It is most extraordinary that practically no policy has been devised on such a revolutionary development. I want to submit that such a policy cannot be pursued by the United States alone, but can best be devised internationally between European countries and the United States." His comment could be applied with equal force to all the wider aspects of this issue.

So far, however, the growing body of literature about these corporations and their foreign activities has been excessively preoccupied with constructing theories and classifications. Once the subject of large companies was adopted by the academic profession, there developed, with an intensity known only to schoolmen, a long and serious debate on the proper jargon to be employed. Credit for coining the phrase "multinational corporation" is generally accorded to David E. Lilienthal in 1960.[5] We have since had codifiers, who have argued in favour of schemes to describe the changing balance in a company as its foreign involvement becomes progressively greater. The proposed jargon has included: national companies, multinational companies and supranational corporations; or multinational, transnational and supranational; or ethnocentric, polycentric and geocentric; all with attendant variations of firm, company, corporation or enterprise.[6] Into such an analytical framework are then placed the progression of companies from a family corner shop to IBM. For those who find their perceptions heightened by such academic scheming, the debate may be of assistance. The plain message is simply that, as companies (corporations, groups, or enterprises) progressively become larger, they fit less comfortably into the framework of our nation states; and they change their character. This change affects those who work for them and affects their relations with governments. It is the size, the market power, the financial power, the bargaining power that matters; not the debate about whether Nestlé is becoming less a Swiss company than BP is a British one.

19

There is an even more substantial body of literature on the "management" of the international company. It is, indeed, a critical problem for the managerial cadres; the problem of how to retain control and yet maintain flexibility; the problem of reducing boredom and fostering a sense of responsibility. There is a new army of professional advisers involved in helping management to solve its difficulties in controlling operations effectively on a scale for which there is no previous industrial precedent. They are primarily concerned with two major themes. The first is the balance between centralisation and local autonomy for the taking of decisions: how far managers down the line or in foreign subsidiaries should have powers to act on their own responsibility. The second is whether the giant corporations should arrange their affairs so that they look at the world in terms of geographic areas, or in terms of products.

Such organisational problems consume a great deal of specialist time. And rightly so, since they must be solved if giant corporations are to continue effective operation. But they are no more than organisational problems. The principles are those that have always been involved in any large-scale operation, conducted simultaneously on different continents, in different countries, through different cultures. On the practical and personal level (how to delegate, how to maintain effective contact, whether to use local staff or fellow nationals), the operations of Esso, with 175 subsidiaries in over 50 countries and selling operations in another 50, are no different from those faced over centuries by the Vatican. Or, on another level, they are no different in kind from those practical problems faced by the men responsible for the giant expeditionary armies of the Second World War. There is now an immense and varied literature on these interesting questions of corporate organisation and management. The main concern of the book, however, is what the international corporations are or could be doing, not the detail of how they are or might be doing it. The main concern is with the substance and content, not with the form, above all where these come into conflict with the wider claims of national identity.

2

An Industrial Revolution

The revolution by which direct manufacturing through subsidiaries in other countries replaced international trade as the main vehicle of economic relations between industrial countries was concentrated in the late 1950s and the 1960s. Certainly, international companies have existed for decades, even centuries. Certainly, foreign capital played a substantial part in the development of commerce and industry in many countries, including the United States.

Even before 1914 such important American industrial concerns as National Cash Register, Woolworth, and Eastman Kodak were active in Europe and elsewhere about the world. Singer Sewing Machines became so much a part of the British Empire that most Englishmen would probably assume that it was a British company. Between the World Wars there was a wave of outward American direct investment, coupled with substantial portfolio investment, particularly in public loans and short-term investments in Weimar Germany. During the Great Depression in the 1930s this portfolio investment was reversed. But the direct American investment in European industry almost maintained its level, with companies like Ford and General Motors realising that they stood a better chance of holding their European markets in this way at a time of economic nationalism and the steady growth of barriers to foreign imports. It was the period when Hoover* was becoming the common noun for a vacuum cleaner in the English branch of the English language.

The surge of foreign investment (both by American and European companies) after the Second World War, however,

* The British subsidiary somewhat eclipsed its American parent company.

21

was so different as to constitute a new phenomenon. First, it was concentrated in other industrial countries: whereas, before, a heavy preponderance had been in colonial territories and areas producing primary products. Secondly, it was concentrated in manufacturing industry, particularly those involving volume production and high technology: whereas, before, the concentration had been in all kinds of mining and in plantations. Thirdly, the volume of the investment was so much higher that it qualified to be considered as something new. And, fourthly, there was a new and deliberate tendency to manage a network of subsidiaries in foreign countries, as if they were an integrated extension of the parent company.

Thus where, for example, today we discuss IBM's integrated computer-making operations round the world, we are talking of something different from the powerful monopoly which the British East India Company enjoyed in British trade with the Orient during the eighteenth century. And, when we talk of Ford's integrated car and truck making operations today, even in Europe, we are talking of a different sort of industrial and economic relationship from the activities of Ford in the United Kingdom and Germany between the World Wars. Or, to take another example, it is true that General Motors bought Vauxhall in Britain and Opel in Germany between the Wars: but these subsidiaries were essentially British and German companies producing British and German cars. They were bought by General Motors because the American corporations wanted a strong foothold in potentially lucrative markets. But by 1970 General Motors were turning Vauxhall and Opel into two integrated components of an international production machine. Some facts and figures outline the revolutionary re-orientation of international industry during the 1960s. In 1954* over 40 per

* By far the fullest figures for direct investment abroad are American. The next best are British. When the European politicians became concerned during the 1960s with American industry's penetration of Europe they argued from American statistics, for they had none of their own. Statistical surveys are published regularly in the United States Department of Commerce's *Survey of Current Business* and in the *British Board of Trade* (now Department of Trade and Industry) *Journal*, e.g. the issue of 23 September 1970. One problem is how to put

cent of all American investment in other countries was in industries directly connected with mining, smelting or petroleum. Almost 70 per cent of that total was invested in Canada and Latin America. By 1969 the entire balance of American investment had changed. In total it had grown almost fourfold. Over 30 per cent of this explosive increase was in Europe. By the end of the decade there was more American investment in Europe than in Canada, which is in many respects industrially part of the United States. And the explosion was in manufacturing industry, related no longer primarily to sources of raw material supply, but to potential markets for industrial products. Well over 40 per cent of all American foreign investment was by then in manufacturing and the greatest share of it was in Europe.

By the close of the 1960s this surge of international investment, for so long dominated by American-based companies, was becoming two-way. On some estimates, up to a quarter of the entire American national output could well be produced by companies under foreign ownership by 1975. Already it is a foreign company, British Petroleum in Alaska, that controls* about half of proven oil reserves in Alaska's North Slope.

Historically, apart from American-based companies, it has been British companies that have contributed most to the rise of foreign direct investment. Even between 1962 and 1968, years of persistent pressure on the British balance of payments and the pound sterling, the book value of British foreign investment

---

an up-to-date value on wholly-owned subsidiaries in foreign countries. These subsidiaries have no share price on the stock market, which could otherwise be used to establish some figure for the total value that the shareholding public, at least, puts on a company. The statisticians are therefore forced back on "book values", the amounts entered in the balance sheet, which normally understate the true present value of the investment. Where foreign direct investment is in a jointly-owned associate company, the book value is usually the original sum of money put up, ignoring subsequent expansion and involving further understatement of true value. American statistics define direct investment as situations where 25 per cent of a foreign company's equity is controlled by an American citizen or corporation, or where 50 per cent of the equity is in the collective hands of American citizens and companies.

* Through Standard Oil of Ohio.

rose from £3,400 million to over £5,500 million, an increase of 64 per cent. The value of British direct *manufacturing* investment overseas (that is not counting the figures for the oil industry, or financial activities like banking and insurance) rose by nearly a third between 1965 and 1968 alone. (The whole weight of this expansion was in other *industrial* countries. Of the £2,180 million increase in the value of investment abroad in the six years to 1968, less than £400 million was in the developing world.)

Indeed, the value of assets owned by British companies abroad grew in this period by more than the sum total of foreign investments owned by Japanese, French, German and Swedish companies put together. British overseas investment today is in fact worth fully a quarter of American foreign investment. In relation to the disproportionate size of the United States economy, this is a measure of the international character of British-based industry.

In those six years to 1968, the value of British investment in the United States itself doubled to £600 million, almost reaching the level of British investment in Canada,* which has long attracted British capital, both because of historical links and because it represents a backdoor into the American market that is outside the full rigour of American rules and regulations. In the same period, British investment in industries in the EEC rose by 130 per cent to £630 million, with the bulk going to Germany and the Netherlands: proof, if any were needed, that industrial and marketing logic, rather than considerations of EEC membership, or the cause of political unity, is the driving force behind investment flows.

The British position is in one respect unique. As well as being a major base for international companies like British Leyland, which make or assemble cars and trucks in sixty countries, Britain is a substantial host to foreign international companies. Over 15 per cent of all British manufacturing industry was by the end of the 1960s owned by foreigners,

---

* £690 million in 1968. British investment in the United States was then 25 per cent more than the total from all the six countries of the EEC combined.

24

with 70 per cent of this figure accounted for by American companies.

The balance between being a base for international companies and being a host to them varies widely from one industrial country to another. While American and British companies dominate the international scene, the most "internationalised" host country is Canada, where the domestic economy has been virtually taken over by foreign companies.*

As early as 1926, some 35 per cent of Canadian manufacturing industry was under foreign control.† By 1963 this figure was already up to 60 per cent. Thus, by the mid-1960s substantially more than half of all Canadian manufacturing industry was under foreign, overwhelmingly American, control. American companies alone controlled over 50 per cent of the Canadian mining and smelting industry. In petroleum and natural gas, the interest of Canadians in their own industry was down to about the 25 per cent mark.

The rest of Europe, Australia and South Africa all have substantial amounts of American investment. For all the political fuss made during the 1960s, France is in fact the EEC member country where the overall penetration of American capital was lowest. This was partly because the climate of Gaullist propaganda produced its effect on the investment decisions of American board rooms and partly because the French has been by long tradition the most protected and autarchic among the major economies of Europe. Thus between 1954 and 1968 the net flow of American direct investment to West German industry was some $3,500 million, while the flow into France was less than half that amount. By the late 1960s, some 13 per cent of French industry's assets were controlled outside France, mainly by companies based in other EEC countries. In terms of relative population, indeed, American investment in the United Kingdom is some two and one-half times heavier than in any EEC country. Within the EEC itself, by that league table France is

* This is also true of less significant industrial countries like Greece and Brazil.

† Measured by the proportion of equity and debt capital of companies under non-resident control to the capital employed in particular industries.[1]

almost at the bottom with less American investment per native than any country except Italy.

Between 1958 and 1963 American companies established or bought no fewer than 3,000 subsidiaries in EEC countries. Italy's estimates are that one in four of the country's large companies are owned by foreigners; with half of those American. In Switzerland in 1941 there were perhaps fifty American subsidiaries. As late as 1950, American investment in Switzerland was worth only some $25 million. By the late 1960s, there were some 650 American subsidiaries in the country, worth about $1,200 million.

Even a country like Spain, so long an industrial backwater, experienced a sudden injection of foreign, again mainly American, capital from 1965, on a scale that will probably produce more fundamental changes in Spanish society over the next fifteen years than have taken place in the last 150. By 1970 well over half of the three hundred biggest American companies were involved with subsidiaries in Spain.

Only Japan has so far been relatively untouched by this revolution. As in so much else, Japanese experience is the exception. For example, by 1968 the value of British investment in Japan, now the second largest economy in the non-Communist world, was valued at a mere £11 million, or about the figure for British investment in a small African country like Malawi. This has been the direct consequence of the strict Japanese limitations on foreign investment. Only IBM and Coca-Cola have been able to get round the regulations against any foreign company having a wholly-owned subsidiary in Japan. Electronics and soft drinks are, exceptionally, two sectors of Japanese industry dominated by foreign capital.

Otherwise foreign investment in Japan has been through joint ventures with Japanese companies, where the non-Japanese share has been kept in the minority. It seems certain that, in due course, Japanese restrictions in this field will be progressively relaxed, if only to meet the need for reciprocal treatment so that Japanese industry can invest freely abroad. Thus, in 1970, restrictions on foreign capital in the Japanese automobile industry were eased. In 1971, as a result, Chrysler set up a joint-venture company with Mitsubishi Motor Industries and General Motors linked with Isuzu Motors. Ford, too, proposed a similar arrangement with Tokyo Kohyo. In each case, to quell domestic worries and the concern of the other two major Japanese manufacturers, Toyota and Nissan, undertakings were given that the American companies would not wholly take over these joint ventures.

The country-by-country pattern of international investment is, therefore, very varied. Equally, the weight of its impact is strikingly concentrated in a handful of industries. The extent of this concentration can be illustrated with a few examples. Some 40 per cent of all American direct investment in France, West Germany and the United Kingdom is owned by Esso, Ford and General Motors. In the reverse direction, well over half of the direct investment in the United States by companies based in EEC countries was provided by a small group of Dutch international giants, notably the Netherlands interests of Shell and Unilever. A 1970 study by the EEC Commission* showed that although, on average in its member countries, American investment varied between 7 and 25 per cent of the total capital stock, the concentration was extreme in certain industries. Thus, American companies control held 95 per cent of the European production of integrated circuits;† 80 per cent of the production of electronic computers (with 65 per cent supplied by IBM alone), 40 per cent of titanium dioxide; 30 per cent of cars and vehicles. This concentration was particularly marked in France, in those advanced technological areas where French industry itself was proving unable to meet the requirements. Although the average penetration of foreign capital in France was, as we have seen, relatively low in the 1960s, the manufacture of photographic equipment was 100 per cent under foreign con-

* See page 50.

† This is the highly sophisticated and expensive technology of producing multiple electronic circuits on minute chips of silicon, which has pushed electronics into the revolutionary post-transistor age. Ninety per cent of European production is controlled by three American companies: Texas Instruments, Motorola and Fairchild Camera.

trol; there was over 90 per cent foreign control in the revolutionary light-weight material carbon fibre and in synthetic rubber; over 70 per cent in ball bearings and agricultural machinery; and over 50 per cent in telecommunications machinery, petrol marketing, lifts and elevators, electric lamps, office machines and car tyres.[2]

And there are other areas of industry where foreign capital is equally concentrated. For example, the European production of numerically controlled machine tools* was by the late 1960s, effectively dominated by two American companies, General Electric and the Cincinatti Milling Group; along with Italian Olivetti, who found this field more profitable than its expensive failure to become a major computer hardware manufacturer itself.

This pattern of concentration by international companies in certain industries and products raises the question why should it be so. In most cases, the answer seems to lie in the nature of the life-cycle of an industrial product. This applies particularly where the product involves high development costs and where the production plant, or machinery, is expensive.

There is a first stage in the selling life of any product, even when it is as sophisticated as a new artificial fibre or an electronic integrated circuit, during which the company concerned can make good profits with a relatively low volume of output and with prices kept as high as possible. If the product is right, it is a seller's market. At this stage, protected by the full paraphernalia of patents and licencing agreements, there is no competition unless other companies develop similar "know-how" themselves.

There comes, however, a second stage in the life-cycle of a product, where the technology involved, particularly the technology of the *production* methods themselves, is developing rapidly. This is a stage where higher profits can be made with lower prices and a larger volume of output. It is the stage where massive amounts of capital are required to expand capacity and where there is a sudden demand for skilled managers and

* Machines performing complex tasks and controlled by pre-set punched tapes.

marketing experts, in place of the earlier predominance of scientists and technicians.

It is in the transfer from the first to the second stage of the cycle that the pressure to "go international" builds up. In the first stage, through initial development, pilot plants, semi-works factories and the first full-scale production, the existing demand should keep ahead of capacity and support a high-price selling strategy. Moving into the second stage, the pressing requirements for capital, managerial talents and expanding markets all make it logical to think in terms of transfering the technology through subsidiaries or joint ventures into other sophisticated industrial countries.

In these terms, for example, at the end of the 1960s, three American companies* had a production lead in marketing electronic integrated circuits in both the United States and abroad of something like a year over any European-based company. And only a handful of European companies were then in a position from which they could ever hope to make up this time lag.†

There is then a final stage in the product's cycle when the patents and other restrictive agreements come to an end, or begin to break down. It is the period when, in comparison with earlier stages, anyone can acquire the necessary "know-how" and anyone can hope to make an impact on the market by aggressive selling and price-cutting. It is in this final stage that there are the strongest pressures towards concentrating an industry in the hands of a few international groups. For, then, costs can only be held down by ever more efficient mass-production, involving huge financial investment in plant and machinery; and the risk of installing all this equipment can only be supported by stable shares of large markets and by stable prices. Competition between a number of firms would result in disastrous price-cutting wars. Since the availability of sufficient capital is the only real restriction on entering the industry at

* Motorola, Fairchild Camera and Texas Instruments. See page 27 above.

† Companies like the British GEC-AEI-English Electric group, or the Dutch Philips concern, or German Siemens, or the Italian SGS.

this stage, existing companies are under continuous pressure to increase their own size to keep out such competition. Since, also, the main manpower requirement at this stage is for unskilled and semi-skilled labour, this is the period when industrial corporations find it attractive and easy to set up new production plants in relatively low wage-cost countries.

Major oil and chemical companies have long since reached this third and final stage of the product cycle. This is why their permanent preoccupation is with their capital financing requirements, for yet more costly refining and other plant, and with maintaining stable markets and market shares. It explains the extraordinary interlocking co-operation, formal and informal, that has developed between them.

Equally, the international motor-car industry has evidently reached this stage. Before 1939, that is before the development of today's mass-production methods, over 50 per cent of all cars sold in continental Europe were either made in the United States, or assembled in Europe from American-made components. Thirty years later, the American motor-car industry, in the hands of General Motors, Ford and Chrysler, had moved physically to Europe. By 1969 less than 1 per cent of cars bought in Europe were made in the United States. And the modern motor-car assembly plant is a good example of how one industry has developed into this flexible, mass-production stage; where almost the only constraint is finding sufficient money to build on the right scale. In 1962 Renault opened its largest and most automated assembly plant, covering some 24 million square feet at Flins, twenty-five miles outside Paris. This was, literally, put down in the middle of a field in an agricultural area where there was no industrial tradition, or labour force. By 1969 it was turning out eighteen hundred cars a day, or over half the company's total production. The eventual labour force was almost wholly unskilled, well over half of it Algerian immigrant labour. In other words, that car plant could, from an industrial point of view, have been established just about anywhere. With the conveyor-belt operation controlled by computer, the craft element in the process had been reduced to maintenance and repair of the plant and machinery. The skills required, after the plant had been designed and built, were managerial.*

It is not often that industrialists can be induced to spell out in simple terms the basis of their international strategy; for they are part of a system that feels a necessity to proclaim the virtues of vigorous competition in industry. In fact, in the sort of industries with which we are here concerned, they know that their lives would be easier and their management more rational, if there were less competition. For expensive plant and machinery need to be run regularly at or near capacity to be economical. What these industrialists would like is an accurate projection of the future market and of their share in it, so as to be able to make plans. The head of one American corporation, however, has publicly stated the reasons why it was committed to being an international enterprise. Tektronix, a dominant manufacturer of electronically-controlled machine tools, followed exactly the three-stage approach to the world market.

In his 1964 annual report to shareholders, the Chairman wrote:

Manufacturing within the major European trading areas lets us provide customers with our instruments at lower prices (by avoiding restrictive trade barriers). It does another thing, it acts to guard our US market against foreign manufacturers, who protected by trade barriers from vigorous competition in their own markets or trade areas could grow strong enough to make inroads here also.

On a still larger scale this has also been exactly the IBM strategy in the world computer market in the post-war period.

If some sort of product cycle theory helps to explain why international companies are concentrated in certain industries, the next question is why there should be such a heavy dominance of *American* corporations in the lists. An answer which Americans are prone to give is that this success reflects the dynamic

* The rubber industry, too, had reached this third and final form of structure by the 1960s. So, during the 1970s, will computers, though by the end of the 1960s IBM had so far established itself that there must be a question mark over whether any company can easily retain or regain sufficient share of the market to support the capital investment costs that will be involved.

quality of the American free-enterprise system. Certainly the whole complex of ideas compressed in that phrase has been, with Marxism, one of the strongest social ideologies of the past two hundred years. There is and can be no positive proof of its economic influence. One can only state one's hunch that it has not in fact had much to do with the growth of American industrial power, whatever Americans may think to the contrary.

The main American advantage, above all in industries associated with advanced technology, has without question been the level of straight government subsidy. More than half of the $25,000 million-worth of orders for electronic equipment of one sort or another in the United States in 1970 were from the Department of Defense, the National Aeronautics and Space Administration (NASA) and the Federal Aviation Agency. Likewise with computers, in 1970 over $2,000 million worth of orders came directly from the government sector. The record in 1970 was just another in the steady year-by-year support given to the industry by government purchasing. With a protected home market of that size, American companies have not found it difficult to develop products that could then be manufactured and marketed in other industrial countries, of a quality and at a price that no non-American company could match. Between 1957 and 1965, the period when micro-electronics was becoming a major industry, over $22,000 million of American tax-payers' money was made available directly for research and development by private United States industry. One intensive survey concluded that "semi-conductors, numerical control, electronic computers . . . as well as a host of less significant innovations owe their development to Federal support."* The OECD also made comparative studies of spending on research and development, country by country, industry by industry, that reveal the remarkable concentration and extent of American public subsidy for science-based industry.†

* From the Organisation for Economic Co-operation and Development (OECD) in Paris on the technological gap between the United States and other industrial countries.

† Conclusions, based on data for 1966–7, were published in *Science Policy News* (Science of Science Foundation) January 1970.

The total figure for spending on research and development by American industry was estimated by the OECD to be worth more than £5,000 million, compared with rough figures of £610 million for the United Kingdom, £510 million for West Germany, £420 million for France and under £300 million for Japan. That is to say, American industry's research and development spending was more than two and one-half times the combined total for all these other industrial countries together. Even making generous allowances for the massive waste with which Americans tackle any large-scale organisational problem, this tidal wave of money thrown at industrial research was bound to show results.*

In a way, however, the most striking fact to emerge from these comparisons is not so much the absolute volume of money spent, but the fact that over half of the total was paid for by the American tax-payer.† It is an under-remarked aspect of the American free-enterprise system that it depends so heavily in ways like this (or the massive tax concessions for the domestic oil industry) on indirect public financing. Government money, in the American case, was found to be heavily concentrated in the aerospace industry which took a third of this research total. This unique injection of tax-payers' money made it possible for American companies to dominate the world aerospace and electronic industries for two decades. The fact, ideologically unpalatable as it may be to some, is that it is only possible to

* In relative terms, as a proportion of gross national product the figure for the United States represented a full 2 per cent, with British industry's spending at 1·6 per cent not far behind, 1·2 per cent for both France and Germany, and 0·8 per cent for Japan. In the Japanese case well under 1 per cent of even this low research effort was financed by government. This reflects the highly successful Japanese industrial strategy of building sophisticated industry by buying the technology involved through licencing or joint-venture agreements with foreign companies. The way in which Sony, for example, starting from scratch, has moved into the world electronics industry is a standing refutation of the argument that, once a national industry falls behind in modern technology, it can never catch up. The Soviet Union has set itself on the same path of buying technology through agreements with international companies during the 1970s.

† Government-financed proportions of these totals spent on research and development by industry were: United States – 54 per cent, France – 37 per cent, United Kingdom – 32 per cent.

sustain industrial activity in these high-cost industries by increasing government involvement.

There are a hundred instances, large and small, of this involvement in American experience. Thus demands from the United States Bureau of the Census in the 1940s did more than anything else to produce pressures for a commercial computer. Demands from the American space programme and, to a lesser extent, from the Vietnam war and other defence expenditure provided the dynamic and financing for science-based industries that the American free-enterprise system could not have generated by itself. Putting a man on the moon cost $23,000 million of American tax-payers' money, with most of it going into the cash flow of American aerospace corporations. The aerospace-programme budget reached a peak of some $6,000 million a year in the mid-1960s. When that annual budget was cut to $3,500 million in 1969 and 1970, coupled with some general reduction in overall defence spending, the impact on the American electronics and aviation industries was nearly calamitous. Areas round Seattle, Washington (something of a Boeing Aircraft Company company town), and most of southern California, known informally as the headquarters of the American military-industrial complex, became employment disaster areas overnight. For the first time, Europeans heard reactions in America identical to those that had come, for example, from British aerospace companies when government funds for projects like TSR2 had been stopped.*

Thus in November 1970 the United States Aerospace Industries Association published a prediction† that employment of skilled scientists and technicians in the aerospace industry

---

* TSR2, which would without question have been the most advanced military strike aircraft in the world, cost some £180 million (including cancellation charges) up to the point where the British Government decided that the project was beyond its justifiable resources.

† Based on data from corporations including Boeing, General Dynamics, General Electric, IBM, Lockheed, McDonnel Douglas, and North American Rockwell, which in itself is something of a roll-call of those who have lived on Federal money.

would drop by 374,000 from the peak in 1968. Karl G. Harr, the Association's President, expressed

particular concern for the breaking up of teams that have been credited with quantum jumps in technological advances in the past two decades. . . . It now appears that lack of projects and piecemeal funding makes it impossible to maintain many innovative development groups with their highly skilled blue-collar support that have given the nation pre-eminence in aviation, space and national security.[3]

The list of those corporations that have benefited by being part of this complex is extensive. It covers General Motors which, besides making heavy duty vehicles and engines for the Defense Department, also has a division in Michigan making M16 rifles and another in Wisconsin making navigation and control systems for spacecraft and missiles. Defence business was averaging some $500 million a year in the late 1960s. Philco-Ford, part of the Ford automobile group, had more than 1,000 employees working for NASA at Houston, Texas, when the first astronaut was landed on the moon in 1969. The corporation was heavily involved in building communications satellites. Two military orders alone netted Philco-Ford over $650 million during the 1960s; for the Shillelagh anti-tank missile and the Chaparrel air-defence system.

If a major reduction in the level of public subsidy for American industry through defence contracts were permanent, it would substantially reduce the balance of advantage presently enjoyed by those American-based international companies. As a lobby, however, the military-industrial complex is more powerful even than the oil industry. And there is the political problem caused by the social and educational class of those being put out of work. As one Nixon administration spokesman was quoted as saying in 1970, "A redundant Ph.D. makes a helluva sight more noise than a sacked fruit picker." A Ph.D. is also less re-employable. It is perhaps for this reason that, in the words of Professor Theodore Levitt, "There is abundant evidence that the American business community has finally, and with un-expected suddenness actively embraced the idea of an inter-ventionist state."[4]

The inevitable meshing of government and industry in order to provide finance for advanced technological industry will be a theme of the 1970s. Looking back at the reasons for the international success of American corporations in these areas in the 1960s, indeed, this factor of access to public finance either directly or through profit on government contracts, seems to have been decisive. In advanced electronics, research and development spending is prohibitive enough, where the sole aim is to protect an existing share of an existing market. To conduct the sort of offensive strategy in foreign markets that we have seen from IBM, or General Electric, or Westinghouse, would not have been possible without that sort of domestic financial cushion. These international corporations have in fact bought their way into European industry in order to exploit more fully the know-how that they have thus been able to develop in the United States.

Yet while American capitalism has adjusted to the idea of substantial dependence on government support, there is little sign yet that the relevant lessons have been drawn, in reverse, by European governments. The case of Rolls-Royce and the British government in 1970 and 1971 illustrates the point at which ideology and technology collide. As air-engine makers, Rolls-Royce rightly enjoyed a reputation without equal. The continuing repute of the company after the War was based on a highly successful series of engines, the Avon Turbojet, the Dart Turbo-prop, the Conway and Spey Turbofans. Rolls-Royce put up over £90 million of its own money to develop these engines and the British Government itself also contributed over £33½ million in recoverable launching aid. The Spey engine alone took £20 million of the company's money to produce.*

There will, for years to come, be a debate about the reasons why Rolls-Royce went bankrupt in 1971. Managerial shortcomings, above all in the area of financial control, certainly

* Even this development expenditure was so large that Rolls-Royce had to adapt its normal accounting procedures. It was too large a sum to be written off in the conventional way against current revenue, for that would have produced a deficit on the profit and loss account which would have destroyed the company's standing with public investors. It was, therefore, treated as a special capital item.

played a major part. So, too, did the fact that Rolls-Royce was badly over-extended in developing three major new engines simultaneously.* In any judgement, however, the mounting cost of developing the RB211 engine must be identified as the major factor. The British government initially put up over £47 million as its contribution in the form of launching aid. This was followed by a further £10 million of public money during 1970 through the instrument of the Industrial Reorganisation Corporation. At the end of 1970, a further rescue package of £60 million was put together. £42 million of this was to come from the government. The remaining £18 million was to come from the Bank of England and from two commercial banks, after an extensive effort by Sir Leslie O'Brien, Governor of the Bank of England, had failed to raise more private money from the banking community.

Part, but only part, of the crisis for Rolls-Royce came from the fact that the company hoped to make substantial weight-savings by using the revolutionary light-weight material, carbon fibre, for the turbine blades. Unable to overcome serious technical problems, Rolls-Royce had to revert to a more conventional design, using titanium.

The truth, however, was that high-risk technology of this sort has gone way beyond the sphere where it can be financed by the conventional methods of private enterprise, industry and banking. This proposition was politically difficult for the newly elected British government, led by Edward Heath. It had a strong ideological and political commitment to reduce government intervention in industry. Brute fact overrode this commitment in February 1971. After evidence of still further financial deterioration at Rolls-Royce, the government decided to cut its losses and allow Rolls-Royce to go into receivership. Despite its political convictions, it was forced to nationalise the dominant air-engine division of Rolls-Royce, thus symbolically underlining the way in which the technology involved has outrun the capacity of private-enterprise organisation.

* RB211 for the Lockheed TriStar, and engines for Concorde and for the Anglo-German-Italian Multi-Role Combat Aircraft.

In a speech during this affair,* John Davies, the Secretary of State for Trade and Industry, indicated the lack of clarity in official thinking on the relationship between government spending and science-based industry. The crucial factor in the government's decision to put money into Rolls-Royce, he said, was the importance of the company to the (British) defence effort and particularly its vital role in keeping the Royal Air Force flying.

To try to pretend that Rolls-Royce is just like any other company is laughable to the point of the ridiculous. . . . It has nearly come to grief in bringing to perfection one of the most complicated pieces of engineering development in the world today. . . . And yet, believe me, the government were not prepared to bail it out willy nilly unless it could show that it could get over its present difficulties and that it could, with a large helping hand at the moment, get through to a profitable future.

The air force of any country will, of course, "keep flying" if it is provided with serviceable aircraft. But Davies was missing a more substantial point: that in areas where development costs are so high, no company can "get through to a profitable future" unless it has access to government financing. Where the sums of money involved in developing each new generation of technical breakthrough rise on something like a geometric scale, no one government with an absolute tax-raising capacity as limited as that of the United Kingdom, France or Germany, can have the political strength to pre-empt the sums required. This means, therefore, that if corporations are to continue functioning in these costly industries, they must become increasingly international; with the ability to sell the next generation of the products to more than one government, or guaranteed market, and to obtain from more than one government the necessary development finance. That is the straight choice for governments with such industries: either to merge their effective sovereignty, or to lose the capacity to support them. In these technological industries, as well, the companies involved must

* At a British electronics industry dinner on 19 November 1970, before the February 1971 crisis which led to Rolls-Royce being placed in the hands of a receiver.

become more international, in order to establish toe-holds in the American market, because that is where the money is.

If governments and management continue to talk in terms of grandiose nationalism, there will be no future for them.* It was a recognition of these pressures that led the British Aircraft Corporation and the French Sud Aviation to co-operate in building Concorde. Only on that basis was there any hope of getting the required, effectively almost open-ended, commitment for finance out of two governments,† or of producing even roughly viable sales forecasts for the supersonic airliner. Both the companies admit privately that the dual arrangement was, managerially, a near disaster. They both declare that it is an experiment that they would never wish to repeat. The same sort of half-hearted shuffle in the direction of internationalism has characterised European scientific co-operation in such thoroughly unmuscular joint projects as the European Launcher Development Organisation (ELDO), the European Space Research Organisation (ESRO) for rockets and space satellites, and Euratom. None of these experiments have produced any results of substance, except irrefutable proof that European governments will have to accept a proper merging of sovereignty and provide common finance for genuinely international and effective companies, if they are to remain in the business at all.

For the companies themselves, the most promising formula is that used for building the Multi-Role Combat Aircraft (MRCA), which is designed to supply the next generation requirements of several European air forces. The MRCA would be the basic creation of two international groups, each with British, German and Italian participation. Panavia, jointly owned by the British Aircraft Corporation, Messerschmitt and Fiat, would build the air-frames. Turbo Union, made up of Rolls-Royce, MAN and Fiat, would build the engines. Both these consortia opened up

* One move in the direction of internationalism for aircraft manufacturers was the merger between the highly successful Dutch Fokker company, whose Friendship (and later Fellowship) aircraft have dominated feeder airlines all over the world, with the German Vereinigte Flugtechnische Werke (VFW).

† In 1962 the original estimated development cost was £160 million. By 1971 this had been revised upwards progressively to £885 million.

the possibility of operating as an integrated multinational group, assured of financing and subsequent orders from three governments at least. A major potential difficulty for the MRCA lies in the development of its electronic systems. For these "avionics" would account for roughly half the total development cost of the aircraft. And, in this part of the project, the arrangements were not the same as those for the air-frame and engine.

This part of the MRCA story again illustrates the way in which, beyond a certain point in high-technology industry, the traditional concepts of intercompany competition have no relevance. For, although in principle it was agreed that the avionic work should be divided between German, British and Italian industry (in the proportion $42\frac{1}{2}$ per cent, $42\frac{1}{2}$ per cent and 15 per cent respectively), there was provision that tenders from companies of other nationality would be accepted, if the price was better.

American electronic companies, increasingly short of good contracts in the United States, were determined to get most of the business, even if it meant quoting what many observers considered to be optimistic terms. Thus Texas Instruments were awarded the contract for the main radar control system, worth at least £80 million, against other American competition, as part of the "German" share. Similarly, the contract for the main flight and weapons control computer was earmarked for the German subsidiary of the American conglomerate, Litton Industries. In this case the "European" competitor was a British Elliott computer, on which joint development work would have been done with Siemens and AEG in Germany.

Much of the pressure to allow direct and indirect American participation in MRCA's avionics came from the German government. In part this was because German industry was in no strong position to play a leading role in the development of the hardware themselves, while the government were happy to buy technology through the licensing process. It is a possible strategy and the one that the Japanese have adopted. It cannot, however, be reconciled with ideas of an independent, advanced aerospace industry for Europe. If such an industry is wanted for the future, it will only be built on the basis of European financial support for European industry. There is no evidence that advanced European technology is any less good at delivering sophisticated developments than the American. Indeed, dollar for dollar, research and development has probably been somewhat more inventive in Western Europe than in the United States. It is worth asking the question what the marketing and pricing policies of American electronics companies in Europe would be, if they once succeeded in cutting all competent European competitors out of business. The outcome of the MRCA affair will be the test of what conclusions European governments have drawn from the evidence about the American government's subsidy for its domestic aerospace industry during the 1960s.

Extensive patronage from the American government, then, has been one major reason for the power of American-based corporations, particularly in science-related industries. On a much broader level, however, American companies have the advantage that comes from being part of the largest-unified market in the world. It gives American-based international companies something of a head start when they transfer their operations to other countries. It was the recognition of this fact that drew so many non-American international companies into the United States during the 1960s.[5] This applied to both ends of the product cycle. For the United States is at once the market where new products are used first and where established products are used most. The market, therefore, attracts investment by a relatively small British electronics company like Plessey and a large petroleum company like BP, or by the large European chemical corporations.

The attractions of the American economy as an industrial market may be illustrated by a few facts. By 1965 there were 105 computers in operation for every 1 million Americans. The comparable figures were 29 for West Germany, 21 for France and the United Kingdom and 19 for the Netherlands and Japan. In the same way, there were 5,000 electronically-controlled machine tools operating in American factories compared with

41

500 in the United Kingdom and 200 in France. Overall, there were three times as many of these machine tools at work in the United States as in the whole of Europe combined. These facts alone explain why corporations like IBM in computers, or Cincinatti Milling Machines, became international with such determination during the 1960s: they wish to be firmly astride this European market when it expands rapidly in the 1970s.

Operating within the United States economy has other advantages, both as a base for American corporations and as a market for non-American international companies. There is the high average income and expenditure of the American citizen. For while only about six people out of every hundred in the world are American, the United States economy produces and consumes something like 40 per cent of the world's total resources. The average American thus produces and consumes something like six and one-half times more than the average human being. The United States represents a concentrated market, equivalent to the total spending power of some 1,300 million "average" consumers. This means that new products or processes (where and by whom invented is no matter) will first be exploited in volume in the American market.*

Rich American consumers also lack the class-conscious resistance to mass-produced items, so prevalent in Europe. In the American market, resources and energy are thus spent much less on producing hand-made items for snob value. It is assumed that there is no essential conflict between mass production and quality. In addition, American business, ever since the great industrial concentrations of the 1890s, has been accustomed to think in continental terms. This gives it a flexibility of approach to the relatively minor administrative problems created by national rules and regulations. To a corporation like Du Pont, used to the tax advantages of being based in the state of Delaware, it comes naturally to think at

---

* Government planners, for example, in Hungary run computerised models simulating current American expenditure patterns, in order to forecast the consumer and industrial requirements for which they must prepare twenty years or more into the future.

once about the possibilities of tax havens in Luxembourg, or in a Swiss canton like Zug.

All these factors are international advantages stemming from the size and character of the American market. They are advantages that to some extent can be and are shared by foreign companies operating in the United States. There is no evidence that large American corporations are inherently more inventive, or that they are responsible for more dynamic industrial decisions. There is, however, a distinction between "invention" and "innovation"; between having a revolutionary idea and bringing it successfully to the market-place. And, in this second area, there is evidence that the American system has devised a flexibility that is lacking in other industrial countries. There is a flux of ideas and men out of large corporations, where they can develop new techniques that would never see the light of day within an industrial giant. Texas Instruments grew in this way, with a Research Director who came from the massive Bell Telephone company. There appears to be both a much greater element of job mobility amongst executives and scientists, coupled with a much freer availability of risk capital to put behind such ventures, than in Europe. Speculative finance in Europe is still firmly in the hands of a conservative and traditional banking community. This is a factor of importance in the early stage of a product's development. And at later stages, when the main requirement is for massive capital and marketing power, the large international group again comes into its own.

Major American corporations are now deliberately entering into agreements for smaller companies to develop new products or techniques under licence, which have been discovered in their own laboratories and research centres, but which they themselves do not wish to develop. General Electric has formalised this scheme to the point where it puts out every two months a publication, *Business Opportunities,* in which it lists industrial ideas that it offers for licensing. National Cash Register and American Standard have set up special departments to perform similar functions. One American oil company, Phillips Petroleum, has made such use of its 6,000-odd active United States patents that the royalties it receives pay for most of the company's research and development costs. There are other flexible links of greater significance. For example, Sherman Fairchild, chairman of Fairchild Camera, is on the board of IBM, which uses Fairchild integrated circuits extensively in its computers.

There is, in short, a flexible combination of money, scientific manpower and new ideas in certain areas of the United States, to an extent that makes up for the inflexibility of the giant corporations. An example is the region around Boston, Massachusetts, where private New England money and the industrial research traditions of the Massachusetts Institute of Technology combined to provide a powerful base for the commercial exploitation of basic defence and aerospace research, at least so long as public funds were available for projects.

These advantages have been combined with an aggressive American dedication to market research for every sort of product from computers to breakfast cereals. This has given American corporations a sharp edge over many of their European rivals, whose approach has been traditionally dominated by the idea that it was enough to produce, in engineering terms, the best aero-engine, motor car, Hovercraft, or machine tool in the world and that the rest would, as a matter of natural justice, look after itself.

Despite this climate of advantage within which American corporations may operate (ranging from indirect government subsidy to the size of the home market), there are industries, even involving the most sophisticated technology, where American companies do not completely dominate the field. These include radar and electronic air- and sea-navigation aids, electronic control and testing equipment, and particular items like electron microscopes. In the "mature" – or consolidated – industries, motor manufacturers like Volkswagen and Fiat, petroleum companies like Shell and BP, and chemical companies like the Swiss CIBA-Geigy, or the German trio of Bayer, Hoechst, and BASF, have demonstrated an ability to do better than hold their own with the international competition. Yet in so many other areas American companies do dominate the international scene.

The final point is that the American market has allowed giant corporations to develop domestically: allowed both in the sense that large organisations were needed for a large demand, and in the sense that American corporations could be absolutely larger within the American economy, without creating fears of monopoly power. The giant corporations that developed within the American domestic economy from the latter part of the nineteenth century were ideally placed to extend their activities across frontiers. Their size created difficulties, in the 1960s, for companies based in continental Europe. For, in almost all the mature industries, the biggest European company is smaller* than any of the top three companies in that same industry, based in the United States. General Motors, Ford and Chrysler are all substantially bigger than Volkswagen. Du Pont, Union Carbide and Proctor & Gamble are all bigger than the German Bayer. Goodyear, Firestone and General Tire and Rubber are all bigger than Italian Pirelli.† In electrical appliances, General Electric, Western Electric and Westinghouse are all bigger than the Dutch Philips. In steel, US Steel and Bethlehem are substantially bigger than the two German groups, August Thyssen Hütte and Krupp. In the oil industry alone is there substantial parity. The Royal Dutch Shell group is second in size only to Standard Oil of New Jersey.‡

Size has become a critical factor for companies operating in established industries. In part this is due to the exploding cost of

---

* Measured by turnover, or assets.

† With the 1970 merger between Pirelli and Dunlop, the combined assets of the group now rival all but Goodyear. The merger is a good example of the industrial pressures for further reducing the number of competing companies in a mature market like motor-car tyres, dominated by a handful of international companies. It remains to be seen whether the two parts of Pirelli-Dunlop can be formed into a corporation that operates effectively in a rationalised way, like the two Anglo-Dutch groups, Shell and Unilever.

‡ The international oil industry is dominated by seven companies known collectively as the "majors", in contrast to the "independents". They are, in order of size, Esso (Standard Oil of New Jersey), Shell, Texaco, Gulf, Mobil, Standard Oil of California and British Petroleum.

developing a new product. The costs directly connected with *invention* may be relatively modest. It is the costs connected with *innovation* (the process of taking a basic research idea and, first, developing it and, then, bringing it to a market) that are becoming prohibitive. There is an effective financial threshold, which a company must be able to cross, if it is to stand any chance of succeeding with an innovation. Once over this threshold and once the new product has been brought to the market, it has a lead over any potential competitors that it can exploit in its pricing and selling strategy.

The height of this threshold, and the length of time during which a company has a quasi-monopoly selling advantage, vary widely. IBM's \$4,500 million development-cost for its System 360 computers has already been noted.* This escalation of development-costs and effort applies, however, not only to electronics. It has happened with equal force, for example, in man-made fibres. It cost Du Pont, the biggest of the American chemical corporations, \$27 million and took them eleven years to bring nylon to the market. But by the standards of later products, even this was a strikingly modest price. Their textile hope in the late 1960s, developed as Fibre Y, and marketed as Qiana, a man-made fibre which has virtually all the appearance and quality of natural silk, with some other advantages besides, took twenty years of research and development, at a cost of \$150 million. Worse still was the fate of their artificial leather material, known as Corfam. Du Pont cut its losses and dropped Corfam in 1971, after eighteen years of development, costing more than \$100 million. Even for Du Pont this was a significant blow. For a small corporation, it would have been intolerable.

Similar factors apply, for different reasons, in technologically uncomplicated sectors like food, tobacco and household detergents. The threshold here is the increasingly prohibitive cost of

* See page 6. The concept of cost thresholds (linked with minimum continuing levels of spending on research and development and lead times for products) is set out for one European industry in C. Freeman, *Research and Development in Electronic Goods*, International Institute for Economic and Social Research, London, 1965.

projecting the image of a new product. The limitation on inter-nationalism in these industries is that a local marketing image is critical; as it is not for petrol, or computers, or man-made fibres. Yet even here there is a growing awareness that differences in national taste are less important than other factors and can be accommodated with reasonable ease.* The real advantages come from co-ordinated production, for which financing comes more easily within a large group. The mass-marketing revolu-tion in food was by the end of the 1960s sweeping over even the French market, that supposed bastion of gastronomic indi-vidualism and the specialised food store.†

With cigarettes, for example, perhaps only one in ten, or one in fifteen, attempts to establish a new brand in fact succeeds. This is the power of a group like British-American Tobacco. It is the second largest cigarette manufacturer, for example, in West Germany, though few Germans would probably know as they smoked brands like HB that these were British products. BAT in Germany puts a new cigarette on the market once or twice each year. This involves a speculative promotional budget that again is more easily financed by a major international group. This is a major part of the explanation for the world marketlng power of Unilever, or Proctor & Gamble, in the admas world of household detergents. At the same time an international group is much better placed to exploit shifts in consumer tastes.

While most observers now accept that, for technical and marketing reasons, we must learn to live with larger industrial empires than have been usual in the past, there are those who consider that the current preoccupation with the consequences

* Thus Kellogg make their celebrated breakfast food All Bran slightly sweeter for the American than the British market, because of the supposedly sweeter tooth of the American citizen.

† This, at least, was the experience of the British company, Brooke Bond, which in 1968 took over the Liebig group, with operations in France, Holland, Italy and Germany. They have found it perfectly practical to produce tinned soups to satisfy every different European taste and foible at one factory in southern France. Other major food groups in Europe like Nestlé, Crown Products, Lipton and Unilever have shown the advantages of international groups in this industry as well.

of size is exaggerated. Lord Kearton, head of the British textile giant, Courtaulds, has expressed his reservations:

I take the view that it is self-evident, in certain industries, that business needs to be big to function effectively. The tables drawn up by the American magazine *Fortune* show that size is closely related to product. Oil, steel, chemical, electrical engineering, motor-car, utilities, even fibre companies, all appear in each nation's big companies lists. And service industries, such as banking and insurance, follow on naturally since they have to be of a size to service the requirements of manufacturing industry. So if the right size for a company is a matter of product, and of fitness for purpose, and of capability in an international as well as a national setting, why should size be a matter for undue emotion, for prejudice, or for fright? . . .

There is no evidence, in any sphere, that size equates with permanency and that great size equates with great permanency. Reflect on the Dinosaurs and on the Mammoth.[6]

Lord Kearton's view was that concentration on sheer size and market dominance of a few companies exaggerates their long-term strength. It was possible, he said, to be over-impressed by the position of "Du Pont in the lush days of nylon". Lord Kearton, in the same speech, said that he "would agree that some of the existing giant companies are probably not far from the tolerable maximum of size." Yet the major international companies and groups involved in these industries confidently expect to become still bigger, either by internal growth, or by taking over competitors. IBM, in computers, looks to a period in the mid-1980s when its total world turnover will have become larger than the economies of Belgium, the Netherlands, Sweden, Spain, Italy or Canada and when it could be in the same league even as Japan. It is only the knowledge of how the anti-trust officials in the United States Department of Justice would react that is stopping General Motors or Ford from trying to take over parts of the Chrysler world-wide network. Other companies, large even in Lord Kearton's terms, are convinced that they must become rapidly larger.

This applies particularly to European-based companies, where the imbalance of their international operations in relation to the size of their home economies is more obvious. By any standard, American or European, British Petroleum is a large company. In comparative turnover, it would be well within the top fifteen of all American corporations. Yet Alastair Down, a BP Deputy Chairman, said unequivocally in 1970, "Unless BP and other important European companies can grow, and grow pretty quickly too, we in Europe are going to be faced with a very disagreeable dilemma." His dilemma was that companies like BP required either greater financial strength to stand up to the power of United States-based companies, or would have increasingly to depend on official protection for their own products in their own markets in order to continue operating. For while size is no guarantee of energy, inventiveness or good management, it is directly related to the ability to protect market interests and raise money.

The size of modern international corporations and, above all, the marketing power that they possess has, in this way, made a qualitative change in the relationship of governments to industry. Any reasonable industrial economy can set up plants of the required size in most cases. The international corporations, however, offer control of markets, without which production is useless. It is increasingly the governments rather than the companies that have become the *demandeurs*; supplicants for the industrial favours being disposed.

Two small examples give a flavour of this change. Shortly before the 1970 British General Election, Nicholas Ridley, then a Conservative Party spokesman on questions of trade and technology,* said in a political speech, "Of course some types of international industry go to those countries which offer them the biggest bribes and it will be necessary for the next Conservative Government to match those inducements." It was a surprisingly explicit statement on the quandary of governments in their relations with international companies, domestic or foreign. They want the new investment and the future expansion, for all

* And subsequently a Minister in Edward Heath's government, acknowledged for a time as one of the leading idealogues in the matter of government policy towards industry.

the advantages they bring directly through jobs and the secondary employment created for the economy in particular regions. These "bribes" in Europe or the United States largely take the form of special grants or other financial inducements offered to investment in economically depressed areas. Ridley underlined his point in the same speech when he went on to say that "industry which is so confined to the United Kingdom because it has to be near its market or its source of raw materials does not need these large grants."

The second example concerns the European Economic Community. In 1970, the EEC Commission completed a study of American companies operating inside the Common Market. The report was confidential; but, as is normal in the workings of the Community, substantial comment and detail soon appeared in the press.[7] The report betrayed that subtle mixture of admiration and jealousy about the supposedly privileged position of American companies that has characterised so much of the European reaction to the new industrial revolution. It has made rational discussion of what is happening, and why, so much more difficult.

This EEC report put with unusual directness, however, the dilemma facing governments of countries the size of those in Europe. It concluded that

In general, it seems relatively easy for American firms to obtain certain tax privileges through agreement with the governments involved. This is undoubtedly because of the economic power of the companies, but mainly because the various member countries of the EEC very much want to improve their competitive position within the wider Common Market. They want to get maximum benefit from the immediate advantages resulting from installation of dynamic foreign companies.

Thus, in order to attract these firms, governments frequently agree to negotiate their tax liabilities. Often such agreements cover not only the tax on company profits and turnover, but also the individual employee's tax liability. . . .

In addition to the loss of tax revenue for the country concerned, which is far from negligible, unequal tax treatment for American and

European companies alters the overall competitive capacity in favour of the American companies. . . .

Anxious to draw maximum benefit from the various advantages consequent on American investment, the member countries compete with one another to squander money and tax revenues and hesitate about trying to formulate a common policy, which would demand patient joint effort.

This is all stated in terms of the relationship between European governments and American-based companies, for such were the terms of reference for the particular study. But, in this context, the American corporation is only a symbol for all large-scale industry that has learned the lessons and advantages of international flexibility in its operations. It is no secret, for example, that the Anglo-Dutch Shell group have led the British government to understand that it would be forced to base most future expansion in the Netherlands, if its operations in the United Kingdom were excessively hampered by official regulations. Shell did indeed transfer its European operations centre from London to The Hague in 1966. Evidence of this operational flexibility for large companies was contained in a booklet[8] published in 1970 in Britain by the Industrial Policy Group, a lobby whose members number the chairmen of many of Britain's largest companies, including ICI, Shell, Dunlop, and Distillers. Although the burden of the booklet was a call for the government to relax controls on direct investment abroad, it had to admit that "no scheme which our member firms 'really' wanted to carry out has been blocked by these restrictions." In the same way the Anglo-Dutch company Unilever, in connection with tactics during a possible take-over,* let the British authorities know that, if its operations were hampered in the United Kingdom, it would concentrate the European expansion of the group on the Dutch half of the concern.

* Of Allied Breweries. Also, during the post-1966 British freeze on all increases in wages, prices and dividend payments, Unilever Ltd asked and received special dispensations from the Treasury, because the company's constitution requires the British holding company Unilever Ltd, and the Dutch company, Unilever NV, to pay the same effective dividend.

There are other similar examples from continental Europe. One concerns the activities of Goodyear, the American tyre manufacturer, in the Grand Duchy of Luxembourg. After the Second World War, Goodyear decided that it would have to manufacture in continental Europe. The Luxembourg government saw the substantial attractions of having a Goodyear plant in the Grand Duchy. For the Luxembourg economy was (and still is) dominated by the iron and steel companies, now combined as a single group called Arbed, and by the revenues from the highly profitable broadcasting success of Radio Luxembourg. The attractions of having such a tyre plant, employing upwards of 2,000 people, were equally clear, however, to the authorities in the Belgian province of Luxembourg, immediately across the border in the Ardennes. Both sides were prepared to make Goodyear extremely attractive offers for the privilege of being given this part of a major tyre-exporting industry.

There were passages almost worthy of Gilbert and Sullivan, as the Goodyear negotiators went back and forth across the border, seeing how far each of the two sides were prepared to go. The plant was, in fact, established in the Grand Duchy in 1951, on terms that effectively gave Goodyear a ten-year holiday from paying tax. With the Luxembourg plant now part of the integrated Goodyear operation, the bulk of the tyres produced there have been exported to Belgium, the Netherlands, Germany, France, Italy and, to some extent also, other markets outside Europe. All this has given Luxembourgers steady employment in the Grand Duchy, together with good foreign-exchange earnings.* In addition, Luxembourg has since 1964 had the advantage of the Goodyear International Technical Centre, which employs some six hundred skilled technicians. There was a similar pattern of bargaining before the Goodyear decision, announced in 1970, to build a second plant in the Grand Duchy.

This pattern is by no means confined to Europe. In Argentina, General Motors have been assembling motor vehicles since 1925. By 1958 the GM subsidiary there was selling GM car

* For these purposes Luxembourg is part of the Belgium-Luxembourg Economic Union (BLEU).

models from the United States and Germany and assembling British Bedford trucks. General Motors then took a decision not to expand its assembly and manufacturing operations in Argentina: it so decided because the low level and quality of Argentinian industrialisation made it unlikely that it could expand these operations efficiently and with profit. But the Argentinian government wanted a domestic motor-car industry and realised that it would have to pay to get it. It, therefore, effectively closed the Argentine market to imported cars and, behind this protective barrier, offered General Motors and others extremely attractive terms. These included duty-free entry for all machinery, tools and equipment required, together with permission to take profits out of Argentina through the "free" foreign-exchange market, so by-passing the less attractive official rate of exchange applied to normal transactions. In return, no less than 40 per cent of each car produced and, in due course, 100 per cent of the engines were to be made in Argentina.* On these attractive terms, General Motors reversed its decision. Today it manufactures, not just assembles, the whole range of Chevrolet cars and commercial vehicles in Argentina.

The fact is that, if a government wants an industry like automobile manufacture, it must come to terms with a major international group. The way in which the international chemical groups established themselves in the industrially depressed area of Northern Ireland is another excellent example; since 1950, Courtaulds, Monsanto, Du Pont, British Enkalon, ICI, BP and Hoechst have made the country into a major chemical and man-made-fibre producer. Attracted as in Northern Ireland, by high unemployment (or by "the availability of trainable labour," as it is euphemistically termed) and by financial concessions from the government, IBM, National Cash Register, Remington Rand, Honeywell, Olivetti and Burroughs Machines have all established plants in Scotland since 1945. The result is that an area previously dependent on contracting industries, like coal and ship-building, is now the most

---

* Australia, Brazil, Mexico and many other countries have used similar techniques to attract and build up local car industries

concentrated computer-producing complex in Europe. In 1945 there was one electronics company in Scotland. In 1970, there were over eighty, employing more than 38,000 people. In the north east region of England, an area of some 20 by 40 miles of an industrial society from another generation, where the level of unemployment is normally not far short of double the national average, there were by 1970 no fewer than fifty-five individual American companies with operating subsidiaries, as a result of an aggressive promotional campaign by local interests. The same pattern applies in some traditional coal-mining areas of continental Europe. General Motors has substantially expanded its Opel plant in the Ruhr; Firestone has extensive capacity at Béthune in Belgium, and Eastman Kodak is active at Chalon-sûr-Saône in France.

If it is true that there is a growing restriction, because of the interests of large international corporations, on the freedom of government policy, the main geographic area where it will be tested during the 1970s looks likely to be Latin America, where there is the combination of heavy direct investment, mainly from the United States in the oil and mining industries, and where there is every probability that national governments with radical policies will wish to re-order existing social and economic structures. The democratic election of a Marxist, Salvador Allende, as President of Chile in 1970 is a symbol of this coming conflict. In part United States industry has already indicated its answer to this probability in the heavy and growing concentration of its foreign investment during the 1960s in politically "safe" areas of the world like Canada and Western Europe.

3

Ideology

"There are few ways in which a man can be more in-
nocently employed than in getting money."
SAMUEL JOHNSON *to* WILLIAM STRAHAN, *27 March 1775*

"The hand mill gives you society with the feudal lord;
the steam mill society with the industrial capitalist."
KARL MARX, *The Poverty of Philosophy*,
chapter 2, second observation

Captains of international industry are wont to think of themselves as pragmatists. They present their corporations as being
innocent of any political motive. They realise that the size of
their corporations disturbs politicians and public opinion in the
countries where they operate. This disturbance, sometimes vague,
sometimes clearly expressed as in Gaullist France, is based on
the notion that they may be less than fully willing to identify
with the aims and policies of local governments; that they will
take without consultation decisions vital to local well-being. To
quiet this disturbance, international corporations, out of enlightened self-interest, take great care to protect their image as
"good corporate citizens" in the countries where they operate.
It is clearly a prudent policy; for, in any country where it
persistently ignored what was locally regarded as the public
interest, a corporation would soon find its activities severely
hampered. This duality has been expressed, albeit in somewhat
mystic terms, by a former chairman of General Motors. "The
world-wide industrial enterprise is a powerful force for economic growth which transcends national boundaries but respects
national goals."[1]

One small, by itself insignificant, event symbolises this readiness to respect national sensibilities. Du Pont, the American chemical giant, with all its European operations directed from Geneva in Switzerland, had three plants in a Belgian town, employing some five hundred people, which made paints, nonstick finishes for items like frying pans, and nylon strapping. The town and the plants were known to Du Pont as Malines. In 1968, at the height of the linguistic and cultural troubles in Belgium, the name was changed on Du Pont maps and charts from Malines, the French name for the town, to the Flemish, Mechelen – "to comply with local usage." It is an example of judicious tact in the face of what, from an American perspective, must have seemed European childishness.

Yet for all this pragmatism, there is a substantial basis of ideology to the growth of these world-wide corporations. They have, necessarily because of their structures, adopted the fundamental ideology of American capitalism. The preponderence of Americans in the lists of international corporations has reinforced this process. The dilemma that this poses for other countries is that of either accepting the values of that society or of cutting themselves off from the institutions that make possible the transfer of American technology between nations.

There was a little ceremony in the United States Department of Commerce at the end of 1970 that illustrates the point. It was to mark the exact moment when, according to statistical calculations, the economy of the United States passed the point where its rate of output was worth more than $1,000,000 million, or one (American) trillion dollars, a year. At the ceremony, attended by President Nixon, Maurice Stans, the Secretary of Commerce and close political friend of the President, delivered what one journalist present described as an ode to American capitalism. "We believe most strongly that the business community itself has the capability and will to eliminate the remaining difficulties that stand in the way of a society that can produce everything that is wanted for the well-being of its people," he said. The phrasing rang a little false in non-American ears at a moment when American capitalism seemed to be facing more sustained problems than at any time since the great inter-war depression; when price inflation itself was in fact the main element pushing the dollar value of national output past the trillion mark, in a period of actual stagnation with high levels of unemployment. It rang false at a time when, to move from the narrowly economic aspects, there were more widespread and deeper doubts within American society itself about the rightness of its values than at any time in the history of the Republic.*

Comparisons between cultures are never easy. And it has certainly never been easy for Europeans to understand the depth of commitment by conventional America to some (not very precisely defined) notion of free enterprise, the notion of the business ethic. One small event indicates the depth that this ethic has sometimes reached. In 1924, a book was published at Indianapolis that remained top of the best-sellers' list for two years. It was a biographical interpretation of the life of Jesus by Bruce Barton. Its title was *The Man Nobody Knows*. Its theme was that the founder of Christianity was the most notable, though unsung, exponent of American promotional techniques. Starting with no capital and only twelve assistants, he had produced an organisation that had flourished for nineteen hundred years. The page following the title page bears the simple quotation "Wist ye not that I must be about my Father's *business*?" This admittedly is an exaggerated instance from the years of pre-Great Depression innocence, but it gives some insight into the ideological basis. And a substantial part has been transferred, inevitably, into the world of the international company.

Since concentration in the hands of a few giant international corporations has proceeded earlier and further with oil and

* These doubts were not just a reflection of the way in which the Vietnam war had damaged the foundations of American society in the 1960s, critical though this was in terms of political division. The social problems, too, of reabsorbing the many ex-GI's returning disillusioned and drug-addicted from the Far East, will have an effect on America in the 1970s which politicians and sociologists have not yet imagined. It was equally a wide questioning of the conventional American wisdom about the effects of their free-enterprise system, a conventional wisdom well captured in those few remarks by Secretary Stans.

motor cars, it is from these industries that it is easiest to find overt expression of the interplay between industrial and economic progress on the one hand, and the free enterprise ethic on the other. It has been expressed thus by Frederick Donner of General Motors: "World-wide industrial enterprise has played an important role in . . . post-war economic advance. It has contributed to the growth of industry wherever market potentials hold promise and national policies were compatible with private enterprise."[2]

Jan Brouwer, as senior managing director of the whole Royal Dutch Shell Group, said the following about the advantages that come from an international company's ability to move people, technology, materials and money to the places where they would make the best commercial return:

One of the most effective vehicles for achieving this mobility and the greater world prosperity that goes with it, is the multinational corporation. Modern means of communications and rapid advances in technology put emphasis on the growing interdependence of nations rather than on individual national economies; on the availability of just one single market rather than a multiplicity of isolated and separate markets.

The multinational corporation and the attendant international investment are part of this new way of life. The nation state in most cases has already become too small a unit to provide a competitive, industrial organisation with an adequately large envelope; hence the last half-century has seen a strong movement towards integration of operations across national frontiers. In economic terms, the nation state's thinking in the past has been based on the idea that products may move internationally, but that the means of production do not. Nations sought to specialise in making and exporting commodities which gave them natural competitive advantage when working from their home base as the sole manufacturing (production) centre.

This has clearly changed. As a propellant towards the economic development of nations and the world as a whole, internationalisation of production has become at least as important as international trade. The multinational corporation, which facilitates the international movement of economic resources and at the same time promotes international trade, is capable of contributing much both to the immediate national interest and to the *more sovereign interest* of world economic development. (My italics.)[3]

58

For the head of the third largest corporate group in the world, at least, there was no doubt that the international company is changing the face of the world. For a Dutchman in that position, a citizen of one of the smaller industrial countries, the disproportionate size and contribution of giant corporations in relation to nation states must be particularly evident. Brouwer was of course generalising from his experience in the oil industry and thus exaggerated the degree to which other industries moved in this direction during the early part of the "last half-century". But he correctly describes the spreading dynamic of the 1960s.

This is an area where the conflict between international corporations and nation states is resolving itself steadily in greater loss of political free choice and effective sovereignty. For the small countries of the Third World this conflict is part of their history. The direct political role of the United Fruit Company in Latin America, by modern standards a small corporation,* or the direct political influence of Firestone since 1926 in Liberia; the detailed involvement of the Belgian Union Minière in Congolese politics, or of an international oil company like Shell in the operations of the Nigerian government during the closing stages of the civil war with Biafra; these are all obvious instances. One of the neatest examples of combined commercial and political involvement, culled from the marginalia of declining British imperialism, concerns Abu Dhabi, the oil sheikhdom where BP and the Compagnie Française des Pétroles have substantial interests. In 1960 Abu Dhabi did not feature on most maps. By 1970 it had the highest *per capita* income in the world. This economic revolution understandably created some social strains in a tribal oasis and fishing village; not least for Sheikh Shakhbut, who had ruled since 1928. In 1966, therefore, he was removed in a palace revolution that had the active prior connivance of the British Government, who were anxious

---

* A good, detailed though completely uncritical record, *The United Fruit Company in Latin America*, by Stacey May and Galow Plaza, was published in 1958 by the National Planning Association as part of a series on United States business performance abroad.

to help discard this individual block to progress and to the increased material well-being of the local people. The full effect of necessary economic and industrial progress on society is illuminated by the following account of that incident:

> Shakhbut was in many ways a good ruler, but he was temperamentally unfitted to bring Abu Dhabi from a desert economy into its oil-rich inheritance. Fundamentally, he did not want to; he did not want to change his people's way of life. . . . His instinct to hasten slowly in all matters of social change was no doubt sound, but his haste was so slow that he became a formidable brake on progress. . . .
>
> His brother Sheikh Zaid, who is much readier to come to terms with the twentieth century, took over the government.[4]

In the case of larger industrial countries, it is not the unreal dummies, set up as reasons for concern about the operations of international companies, that are important, though some, like their commercial and financial policies, have significance. The real limitation comes from the fact that a nation state has to provide the sort of political, social and financial climate in which these corporations are happy. For practical purposes there is no choice. And where there is no choice there is no sovereignty.

Brouwer, in that lecture, explicitly made the point about a divergence between national interest and "the more sovereign interest of world economic development." The multinational corporation, he went on,

> is a new form of social architecture, matching the world-girdling potential inherent in modern technology; an economic and technical phenomenon inherent in modern life, and which increasingly pervades all aspects of national and international economies. . . .
>
> In an age when modern technology has shrunk the world, and brought us all closer together, the multinational corporation and the nation state must get used to living with each other.

Yet, in the long run, this is a merging that will take place on the terms that suit the international corporations. They are terms that will determine in the most fundamental way possible the priorities and the values of our societies. For international companies to operate willingly in a proper climate of commercial profit, Brouwer said,

there is an absolute need for everyone, not least the government, to see to it that every activity in the economic sector of the country's household should if at all possible lead to a growth in the GNP.* Under that conception such economic activity should be encouraged in direct proportion with its GNP contribution; thereby it should earn and receive its social sanctification.

That is a strong statement of the view that what is good for Shell is good for mankind. The same view, generalising from a case study of General Motors, was put by the Dean of the Graduate Business School at Columbia University:

The experience of General Motors in its overseas business has, with appropriate variations, been duplicated many times by business corporations of many nations. The resulting global pattern of mutual interests and associations cuts across national boundaries and constitutes an interwoven network for the transfer of knowledge, administrative skill and technical competence that cannot fail to be progressively more meaningful in man's search for a better way of life.[5]

There is no real trace of mass revolutionary rejection in any European country, East or West, of the materialist ethic contained in these quotations. In that absence, governments and their people will find it increasingly difficult to put forward any alternative that carries conviction. The dilemma is that increasingly, with the American example before us, people are beginning to have doubts about the social consequences that are the obverse of an economic system, whose fruits are still desired.

It is a matter for regret that political scientists, as a group, provide few plausible explanations of anything but the blindingly obvious. But there does seem to be a thread running through events like the political disturbances in France during May and June 1968, which came close to toppling General de Gaulle; the widespread German student disturbances just before; the running industrial strife in Italy between 1969 and 1971; the

* Gross National Product.

universal "hippie" movement; or, symbolically, the ritual self-disembowelling at Tokyo in 1970 of the Japanese extreme patriot and poet, Yukio Mishima. They seem all part of a rejection of the gods of materialism and modern industrial efficiency. But these are, and seem likely to remain, minority manifestations. Politicians tend to pay more regard to majorities.

To most people it might seem extravagant to suggest that social attitudes are so affected by guiding philosophies of industry and business. And yet basic optimism about the ability of a liberal society to absorb any amount of economic and industrial change and still maintain its values has, at least, to be questioned. Such questioning might, for example, centre on educational experiments like the new British University at Warwick.*

The boast of the first Vice-Chancellor, J. B. Butterworth, was that he would create a university tailored to the needs of an industrial society. It was on this basis that Butterworth, an academic lawyer of ambition and energy, raised funds with great success for his University. Butterworth was particularly successful in getting endowments from commerce and industry, including the Barclays Bank Chair of Management Information Systems, the Clarkson Chair of Marketing and Economics, the Volkswagen Chair of German, the Institute of Directors Chair of Business Studies, and a Chair of Industrial Relations, endowed by Pressed Steel Fisher, part of the British Leyland Motor Corporation. It would be quite unfair to suggest that any of these sponsors directly affected the workings of the university, except in so far as rather more money may have been spent on science and technology than was warranted by the proportion of undergraduates studying these courses.

---

* In February 1970 the University was for a while something of a national *cause célèbre* when students, having invaded the University registry, found a confidential report on the political activities of a visiting American professor, Dr D. Montgomery. This report was apparently prepared for the Vice-Chancellor by the Director of Legal Affairs of the Rootes Organisation, the British subsidiary of the American Chrysler Corporation. The report concluded that Montgomery had said nothing at a local political meeting that could involve prosecution under the 1919 Aliens Registration Act.

Less conventional, however, in terms of normal academic disciplines, have been the direct links with British and other corporations. Thus, at one time or another, the University has done research on metal fatigue that was of interest to a Canadian subsidiary, Massey-Ferguson; on vehicle instrumentation, of interest to Chrysler and Ford; on tyre fatigue of interest to Dunlop, and on the manufacture of high-speed machine tools, of interest to Alfred Herbert. The business orientation of Warwick was further underlined by the composition of the Council, the University's governing body. At the beginning of 1970, of the nine co-opted laymen on this body, from outside the University, one was the Bishop of Coventry, and the others were all prominent businessmen. These included the Chairman of a machine-tool manufacturing subsidiary of Tube Investments,* the Chief Executive of Rootes (now Chrysler UK), the Vice-Chairman of Barclays Bank and the Chairman of Alfred Herbert. Though not concerned with day-to-day administration, such a governing body sets a tone and affects marginal decisions that can cumulatively be significant for any institution, be it a university, a newspaper or a company.

In 1968, the University Council engaged a firm of industrial consultants, John Tyzack & Partners, to look at its operations. Their report concluded that "taken as a whole, the University is certainly inefficient by normal commercial or industrial standards." It recommended that the overworked Vice-Chancellor should have a deputy, whose position should not carry with it the security of normal academic tenure, because "this is primarily an administrative appointment, and we see no reason why it should not be treated by Council in the same way as a board of directors would treat the appointment of a general manager."

The report contained, according to versions that appeared in the press,[6] several other passages comparing university practice with efficient business, which found academica wanting:

We have been told that democracy has a special place in University life and that there is constant political pressure from the rank and

* Coventry Gauge.

file of the academic staff claiming the right not only to be consulted more but to "have a hand in decision making". The result in practice is already an amorphous and time-wasting system which has led to needlessly protracted argument, dilatoriness in the taking of decisions, uncertainty regarding the effectiveness of power and action, and at times to conflicts of policy. . . .

Sooner or later the University of Warwick will have to come to terms with the age-old conflict between democratic principles and effective government. . . .

Committees absorb not only the energies of salaried members of the academic staff whose primary function is supposed to be teaching and research, but also the time of registry staff who have to service the committees.

It is the assumption inherent in that report that the values and organisation of efficient industry are overridingly superior in every context, which is the most disturbing element. It is a system of values to which our societies are ever more attracted, because of our desires for material affluence; a system by which we increasingly allocate "social sanctification". The role of education, in particular higher education, in society is a much wider question than that posed by Butterworth's Warwick. There are already a whole range of pressures for a more "utilitarian" approach to education. It would seem, however, curious that anyone should start from the assumption that the best structure for institutions of learning is the value system of modern industry and capitalism. A more reasonable starting point, at least, might be that such a system, outside its proper place, should be constantly questioned, if civilized society is to survive the impact of the industrial institutions about us.

4

A Matter of Identity

"After discussing the weather in hand-signal Amharic, bargaining in guide-book Turkish, and getting directions in dictionary Hebrew, its nice to go back to a Hilton where everyone speaks your language and where holding a conference is as easy as at home."

Advertisement for HILTON HOTELS

International corporations during the 1960s have created a new, rootless culture. It is based essentially on those things that a middle-class American executive likes to have and see around him, when he is away from home and someone else is paying the bills. For the spread of industry in physical disregard of national boundaries has inevitably been matched by changed working habits for corporation managements, by developing a sub-population of executives in semi-permanent orbit. To be sure, businessmen travelled before. But, just as the bulk of international commerce was then in exports and is now in physical production, so then most of the business travellers were salesmen and are now increasingly managers concerned with production and all its associated problems.

It is the world of the new jet set: not of the gilded and the idle with time and leisure to travel in search of the sun, but the cohorts of middle and senior management, hurrying from city centre to airport, from airport to city centre, on the business of their corporate masters. As the great industrial empires grow and at the same time become more integrated, there is an ever increasing requirement for annual meetings, co-ordination meetings, regional meetings, in order to preserve the minimum tolerably efficient level of personal contacts. The wonders of the modern telephone, telex and communications satellite will never meet this need. The result has been a bonanza for all the service industries, airlines, hotels, car-hire and credit-card companies that cater directly to the needs of this group. They are the needs of a man who is travelling, but has neither the time, nor the inclination, to appreciate the dwindling cultural differences between the places on his circumscribed route; a man with virtually* no limit on the amount that it all costs.

The permanent (or semi-permanent) migrations of expatriate managers are relatively unimportant. International companies, even the American-based ones, were rapidly finding during the 1960s that it was more effective and much cheaper to use native management, properly imbued with zeal for the corporation concerned, than to post large numbers of their own nationals for long periods of service in other countries. There are perhaps as few as 75,000 American businessmen based and working abroad for some 4,500 American subsidiaries. These postings will certainly continue, particularly for the earlier stages of a new operation. But the trend is to limit them to a few key personnel; above all, to chief executives and finance-controllers.†

Numerically, it is the quick business trip that dominates air travel. One airline operating in Europe, British European Airways, is quite clear that business travel has been responsible for the industry's swift expansion. The flight schedules on popular

* Defined as company policy on expenses.

† International companies of other nationality seem to be moving, with variations, in this general direction. Thus the European operations of ICI, integrated through the Brussels-based office of ICI Europa, employs less than 2 per cent of United Kingdom based staff in the managerial complement of some six thousand. It is also trying to move executives about to third countries, so that a German ICI manager might be working in the Netherlands and vice versa. Although in absolute terms these "third-country nationals" are in a very small minority, the company stated in 1969 that it was "ICI policy to increase the scope for such moves within the Group so that valuable international experience can be gained and talent used in the Group's overall interest." For a start in 1970, of the eight senior management posts with ICI Europa in Brussels, one was held by an Argentinian, one by a Frenchman and one by a Dutchman.

66

routes for businessmen* are arranged to suit the needs of those who want to get to a mid-morning meeting, or back from one in the afternoon; as anyone discovers who wishes, for some eccentric reason, to travel during the middle of the day. European airlines are finding that something like half of their total passenger load is made up of men on business. In 1970 BEA estimated businessmen at 60 per cent in their North and East Europe region of operations. The concentrated flow of this new traffic, like the concentration of foreign investment, is between Europe and the United States. Homogenised airline travel, where service and not price competition is the only concern, and where the service seems virtually identical beyond the clothes of the hostesses, is a pointer to the direction in which this whole industrial revolution is moving.

International Telephone and Telegraph, the thriving American conglomeration of international interests, has rapidly spread beyond the manufacture of telephones and communications into this area of direct personal service. Hotels and consumer services accounted for 15 per cent of the total ITT income in the mid-1960s. By 1970 this figure was up to 37 per cent. In Latin America, ITT even used to advantage the blow of having some of its telecommunication interests nationalised. In Peru the compensation money was used for a hotel in Lima.

ITT's major step in this direction was to take over the international Sheraton Hotels group in 1967. For an estimated $200 million, it got hotels in fifteen countries and a minority interest in the Diners Club. It also owns the Avis car-hire company. And all of this gives the conglomerate a solid and integrated position in the cashless, fly-and-drive world of the international executive. The advantage of these arrangements is that each activity advertises and sells the other, to provide a complete cocoon within which the businessman away from home can move with least distraction from different national idiosyncracies. It is above all for this reason that the airlines themselves have been drawn into the hotel business. Pan

* In the BEA case, for example, between London and Brussels, Hamburg, Düsseldorf, Copenhagen, Paris, Turin or Milan.

American started the Inter-Continental chain, initially in Latin America, after the war. Since 1961 it has expanded rapidly in Europe and elsewhere; and by 1970 Inter-Continental had 48 luxury hotels about the globe. TWA bought Hilton International in 1967 as its stake in cultureless living for the 1970s.

In 1970 Hilton International had 53 hotels and plans for some 20 more. Sheraton were aiming for 41 hotels in 38 foreign countries by 1973. BOAC, the British international carrier, has some direct hotel investments, but in the 1960s concentrated mainly on co-operation with Pan American and its Inter-Continental hotels. British European Airways, on the other hand, has been closely associated with Fortes, the British hotel group.* Together, for example, they run the Georges V, that landmark amongst hotels in Paris. All the major airlines are moving rapidly in this direction. Even Air India will build two international hotels at Bombay in the 1970s.†

This explosion of business travel has given the neo-"Grand Hotel" an enormous boost. It has, however, ensured that the main development takes place in a particular direction. Such hotels, to be profitable, now have to stress their international brand image; to provide as uniform a service as possible so that the businessman can be referred onward by computerised reservation systems from one link in the chain to another without disturbances. All Sheraton hotels, for example, are linked by direct line to a $4 million computer in New York, Reservatron II, which handles bookings for the group's world-wide total of 45,000 similar bedrooms. It is the security of sameness that their international clientele desires, not the stimulus of change.

To see the great ebb and flow of businessmen, it is only necessary to sit for a while in an international airport, counting those metal-rimmed, black despatch cases that have become the

* Fortes merged its interests with Trust Houses to form Trust Houses Fortes in 1970.
† It is the air-travel equivalent of the revolution that the motor car produced in the United States, supporting chains like Holiday Inns, Travelodge and Howard Johnson. Esso are still probably, in terms of motels, the major American investor in the European hotel industry.

badge of the significant corporation executive. The impression is confirmed by the experience of individual companies. A typical example of the new-style international empire is the British-based mining and metals group, Rio Tinto-Zinc, built up into an international group with a combined annual turnover of some £340 million by its Chairman, Sir Val Duncan. Some 10 per cent of the group's senior London-based executives are out of the country on business at any one moment. This figure is matched by management travelling elsewhere within the group. For American executives, with their cultural propensity for conferences and symposia, the pressure and the distances are even greater. Jacques Maisonrouge, the young French president in charge of all IBM's integrated overseas operations, is travelling abroad, away from his New York office, for six months out of every twelve. His annual programme is only an exaggeration of the pattern common to the international businessman.

Catering for the needs of this population in orbit has directly affected the quality of building in major industrial cities. Giant international hotels have taken the place of great cathedrals in another era as the architectural show pieces of the urban landscape. Hotel-building plans in London alone will quadruple the number of beds available during the 1970s. These beds have become greatly more expensive in the process. The cheapest single room at the London Hilton in 1970 cost £10 a night, with other international group prices for major cities in the same sort of range. The reason is, quite simply, that only about one in five of the guests is paying his own bill. Consequently, there is little pressure to keep prices down. The hotel boom has also introduced deliberate planned obsolescence for the first time into major urban architecture. For hotels in this class can only be kept profitable by constant modernisation, to reduce the impact of ever-rising labour costs. It has become cheaper to pull down and rebuild, than to undertake the fundamental reconstruction of an existing shell. The life of a new "Grand Hotel" today may not be much more than thirty years. It makes an interesting comparison, in the British case, that plans for rebuilding the splendid and wholly archaic government buildings of Whitehall have had to be shelved for decades because of the cost; while a hotel may now be pulled down and rebuilt three times within the life-span of a Londoner. *Sic transit gloria mundi*.

One way in which to capture the quality of this international business world is to look at the magazines that are prepared for the market. One such, *Vision*, which describes itself as the European business magazine, was almost entirely supported by advertising from international companies when it appeared in 1970. With the limitations of national newspapers and periodicals, these corporations have no medium through which their prestige advertising can currently reach people in several countries at once. During the 1960s the only vehicles were, in fact, glossy American magazines, like *Business Week*, published weekly by McGraw-Hill, and to some extent the international edition of the *Herald-Tribune*, published daily on the Continent. The advertising response for the first edition of *Vision* demonstrated the need that these corporations feel to explain themselves to a certain supranational readership. They were led by Westinghouse, followed by the First National City Bank of New York. Then came a clutch of airlines, Pan Am, Lufthansa, Air France, Eastern Airlines, TWA and BOAC. The British Aircraft Corporation was there, announcing that "it recognises no boundaries in aerospace." And then, interspersed with all the good things of life, like Canadian whisky, Scotch whisky, Marlboro cigarettes and Rolex watches, there followed a representative cross-sample of international industry and commerce, Bank of America, Standard Oil of New Jersey, Singer, Borg-Warner, Chemical Bank of New York, Rank Xerox, Chase Manhattan Bank, General Electric, Sheraton Hotels, Olivetti, Mannesmann, Fiat, Rhône-Poulenc, Badische Anilin (BASF), Mack Trucks.

The appearance of magazines like *Vision* underlines one major social consequence of the international corporation It. has ensured the total dominance of English as the language of international business and its position as the future lingua franca. The fight to preserve something like parity of status for the French language, a strong element of Gaullist political strategy, has been lost.* This element informed General de Gaulle's views on French Canada; an island of Gallic civilisation in the very heart of North America, bearing something of the relation to Paris that Albania does to Peking. If that linguistic struggle ever had a chance of success, the growth of the international corporation has killed it. It was not so much the spread of American corporations in Europe and elsewhere that decided the day. In the last resort it was the acceptance by non-American companies themselves that they must become increasingly international, must adopt the intercontinental management style, that ended any chance of linguistic autarchy. The change is, as might be expected, most marked in France itself.

For it was the Frenchman who reacted most vigorously against the extraordinary linguistic and cultural arrogance with which the average American goes upon his way about the world. With notably few exceptions, the American businessman has shown no willingness to make concessions to other cultures, either in the question of language or of money. He expects English and the dollar bill to be understood and accepted in every corner of the world. Consequently, in general, they have been. It is an arrogance only matched in recent times by the British in the nineteenth century. Thus it was that, even in the early 1960s, the French educated and managerial classes would make a deliberate point of not speaking English, unless it was totally unavoidable. By the end of the 1960s, the entire balance had changed. The evidence can only be impressionistic: but it is striking how senior French management has developed an

* Stout cultural rearguard actions, however, continue. The April 1971 issue of the respected *Revue des deux mondes*, for example, contained a long article by Pierre Laurent entitled "La langue française dans le monde", which was a rallying cry to the defence of the French language. The instinctive way in which Frenchmen identify together the use of their tongue and the course of civilisation is a source of constant surprise to non-Frenchmen. When Mr Heath and President Pompidou met in Paris in 1971 to decide whether France would support British membership of the European Common Market, the British Prime Minister gave a confidential undertaking that all British officials (not just diplomats), who would work in the community sphere, would be able to do business in French. For the French, this was a major concession.

almost embarrassing eagerness to demonstrate a command of the English language. The last dyke has broken.

This sudden expansion of English as the working language of ambitious executives was naturally assisted by the initial predominance of American and British subsidiaries in the wave of foreign direct investment. As international companies increasingly employed local management, more and more of these executives in Europe were required to communicate with their head offices in English. Then, however, the process became two-way. For, when non-Anglo-Saxon corporations "went international" as well, they had to adjust to the fact that English, since the War, had become the language of international commerce and finance. In those companies, too, where senior and middle management, above all in head and regional offices, was becoming more polyglot, English filled the role of the natural common language. When two or more diplomats of widely different backgrounds are gathered together, French is still, though decreasingly, the most likely common tongue. With businessmen, it is now certainly English.

A handful of European companies have drawn the final conclusion on the language question. The Swedish company, Svenska Kullagerfabriken (SKF), international manufacturers of ball bearings, roller bearings and other steel products, has made English the official company language for its head office announcements, official publications and all correspondence involving more than one of its subsidiaries. The Netherlands-based Philips concern has gone even further and made English the language for all internal correspondence. These companies are in the van of a movement that has done more to spread the English language than the combined efforts of the United States Information Service and the British Council could possibly have done.

In this process of making management as international as the companies for which they work, a key role has been played by the business schools. Lineal descendants of the great Harvard Business School at Cambridge, Massachusetts, they have been the main vehicle for conveying American business techniques and attitudes to management in other countries. At the same time, they have been the vehicle for creating a management élite, whose professional pride and standing is increasingly divorced from any particular national framework: so that French executives, for example, are so trained that they feel more at home in working for a good American computer manufacturer in France than for a bad French one. It is a managerial cadre, trained to put the commercial interests of their corporation above other considerations. These business schools, or university departments, now exist all over Europe, from Norway to Spain and from Ireland to Czechoslavakia. For the new management attitudes are no respecters of the superficial differences of politics.

During the 1970s the top management of large non-American corporations will increasingly be the successful alumni of institutions like the European Institute of Business Administration (INSEAD) at Fontainbleau near Paris, or the Centre d'Études Industrielles (CEI) at Geneva and the Institut pour l'Études des Méthodes de Direction de l'Enterprise (IMEDE) at Lausanne, or their British counterparts at London and Manchester. There are variations like the Spanish Instituto de Estudios Superiores de la Empressa (IESE), attached to the University of Navarra at Barcelona, which aggressively conducts all instruction in Spanish in the hope that it will be possible to produce a home-spun model of the international businessman.* For the most part, however, the ethos is decidedly American. The business schools think of themselves as the staff colleges, or perhaps the guerilla training schools, for the future campaigns of international management. They are heavily supported by the great international corporations. CEI for example was sponsored by Canada's largest industrial company, Alcan Aluminium. IMEDE was founded by Nestlé.

The present generation of top management in Europe began their careers before the business-school revolution was under

---

* The first batch of Masters of Business Administration graduated in June 1966 from this place, which has close connections with the radical Catholic Opus Dei movement.

way, except in the United States.* The next generation are being equipped with a confidence that they have the techniques and ability to be good managers in any circumstances. They know that in business, as in everything else, there may be substantial differences of detail from country to country, summed up in the old saw that "In France all things are permitted and nothing is possible; in Italy nothing is permitted and all things are possible." Yet they are being equipped, like the products of the British private-school system in earlier decades, with that inner conviction that they will know how to handle the levers of power in all circumstances: in short, that they are an international élite.

Yet, while it is clear that this is to be the basic career structure for executives in large international corporations, there are severe personnel problems that will have to be faced and solved in the next generation. They centre on the fact that large-scale industry is, inevitably, bureaucratic and depersonalised. The career structure that it demands has more in common with the pattern of government service, with all its strengths and weaknesses of security and *esprit de corps*, than with more traditional ideas of the entrepreneur. Gone are the days, in large-scale industry, when an individual could so dominate the commanding heights of industry. The great Standard Oil trust was in a real sense the creature of John D. Rockefeller's personal mixture of genius and unbending ruthlessness. The growth of Ford was the industrial expression of the energy and ambition of a third-generation Irish immigrant, Henry Ford. In 1927 the ferocious oil-price war, which largely convinced the major companies that their best interests lay in mutual co-operation, broke out between Shell and Standard Oil of New York, because Henri Deterding of Shell, whose wife was an exiled Russian aristocrat, objected to Standard's buying Soviet crude oil and selling it in India.[1]

* Business schools, out of enlightened self-interest, have done a good deal to sell themselves to these senior executives. CEI, for example, organised the first European Management Symposium for five hundred top European executives in early 1971 at the fashionable Swiss ski resort of Davos. For an all-in fee of about £700, the programme included talks by Herman Kahn, J. K. Galbraith, Jacques Maisonrouge and Jean Rey.

In 1929 the Netherlands Margarine Unie merged with Lever Brothers to form Unilever, rather than come to some other market-sharing agreement, at the critical moment largely because "it had been a long standing ambition of Mr Anton Jurgens to be associated in business with Lever Brothers."[2]

It would be difficult to claim that a large-scale international corporation was run on such personal lines in the 1970s. For, while to some extent the mythology of the great entrepreneurial age has been passed down to the present generation of senior management, it accords less and less with reality. There are corners, particularly in Europe, where the old pattern lingers: like the interlocking industrial empire controlled by the Wallenberg family in Sweden,* or the personal stake of the Belgian Baron Empain (the heir to the family that financed the building of the Paris Metro) in industrial groups like Jeumont-Schneider in France. But these are shrinking islands of personal identification in the large industrial groups of today; islands being submerged by the managerial tide. The great industrial institutions have a corporate impetus of their own. The managers who are their servants may be as concerned to make profits as the entrepreneurs of a former age, but their relationship to their corporation is very different.

For the industrial giants are now too complex to be run on a personal basis. Control devolves inevitably upon a structure of executive and co-ordinating boards and committees. Some American corporations have even taken the further step of deciding that their activities are too complex to be handled effectively by one chief. Both Westinghouse and General Electric have tried the experiment of not having a single, conventionally paramount President. Westinghouse now has two Vice-Chairmen to whom substantial amounts of the President's authority have been delegated. General Electric has tried a system where a Chairman and three Vice-Chairmen share

* This hundred-year-old family group has substantial interests in eight of the ten biggest industrial concerns in Sweden. The present patriarch, Marc Wallenberg, is President of the Enskilda Bank in Stockholm and simultaneously Chairman of Scandinavian Airlines (SAS), Volvo and Saab, and of the international manufacturers of compressors and pneumatic drilling equipment, Atlas Copco.

authority together. This idea of having an "Office of the President", but no single president, seems likely to spread.

This growing pattern of somewhat anonymous service to a corporation is revealed when, in the papers, biographical details are given for those being promoted to higher management levels. In the big corporations, the top jobs are now going with increasing regularity to those who have worked their way up through a life-time of service to the same group. One example is enough to make the point. A recent General Motors annual report carried for its shareholders a list of the top nineteen group vice-presidents and senior staff officers. Of these, 13 had worked for General Motors for more than 30 years, 3 for over 40 years. Only 3 had been on the General Motors payroll for less than 10 years. That General Motors should wish to stress this sort of biographical information in its annual report is a reflection of the attitude that it is an institution which a young man joins in the expectation of spending a lifetime in its service. This says nothing about the general ability of those who rise through the system to run these giant corporations. It is, however, a system which ensures that it is the safe man, the committee man, the natural diplomat or politician, who rises highest. The problem that these corporations now face is how to recruit and continue to motivate management of the right quality to run such industrial bureaucracies, when they have to recruit from a generation of affluence, education and independence that remembers nothing of job insecurity between the Wars. Those who run the major business schools are under no illusions but that their task is to create properly motivated recruits for the system.

Many of the brighter and younger of today's businessmen also react against all the paraphernalia of office status symbols (who gets office carpets, and of what quality and size) that are making day-to-day working within large corporations like a music-nall version of life in a government department.

As many giant international corporations are beginning to realise, the monolithic structure of the modern corporation risks repelling the very sort of bright managerial intake required to keep the structure alive. A symbol of this was the decision by six directors of a relatively small British insurance company, Abbey Life Assurance, to resign when it was taken over in 1970 by the American conglomerate, International Telephone and Telegraph. "It is," said the managing director Mark Weinberg, who had created the business personally, "jolly difficult . . . to have to act according to someone else's rules." The business schools of Europe are also finding evidence that their best students gravitate within a few years towards the smaller rather than the larger companies, because they wish to feel that their talents are being exercised in a way that produces some visible effect. There is also some rejection amongst potential executive recruits of the overt American enthusiasm for business as an end in itself, an attitude that has carried over into international companies.

A large corporation like Shell showed itself sufficiently exercised by this problem during 1970 to institute seminars between senior personnel management and some of London's more revolutionary students. Most said that they would never think of joining an organisation like Shell. One said that it was worth joining to subvert the company from within.*

The point of this growing unsureness of touch and purpose in giant corporations was well put by Paul Jennings of the AFL-CIO to a United States congressional committee:

What's good for General Motors is *not necessarily* good for the USA. What's good for Mitsubishi or Toshiba is *not necessarily* good for Japan. What's good for Lever Brothers is *not necessarily* good for the United Kingdom. What's good for SKF is *not necessarily* good for Sweden. What's good for Massey Ferguson is *not necessarily*

* Shell management is particularly sensitive to the charge that the giant corporation cramps individualism. In a letter to *The Times* (30 April 1971) Sir David Barran, Chairman of Shell in the United Kingdom, reacted sharply to a leading article which had made a passing link between the oppressive materialism of the massive Shell Centre on London's South Bank and the raising of battery hens. "Size is a phenomenon with which we as a society will have increasingly to cope. . . . Size can be properly used, and when so used it puts greater skills and greater capital equipment into the hands of each member of an organisation, calling for greater, not less, responsibility and initiative."

good for Canada. In fact, the new developments these changes bring about may show that General Motors *doesn't know* what's good for General Motors etc. much less for the USA etc.

In this predicament the major international corporations are, in an ill-defined way, seeking a new image for themselves, an image required quite as much internally as externally. It seems that they have chosen the notion of "service". In place of the idea that their proper function and pride is to make profits, many are consciously trying to project the idea that they are just the servants of mankind. Thus, when, in 1970, ITT wished to celebrate its fiftieth anniversary with an advertising campaign, the burden of its message was not its half-century of successful expansion, profit and return to its shareholders as an international conglomerate. It was, instead, the fifty years of "ITT – serving people and nations everywhere," "a multinational corporation helping to make the world's resources more useful to the world's people." Or Donner, on the reasons why General Motors' shares should be on sale and freely available in more parts of the world:

Our desire to broaden our base of ownership is consistent with General Motors world-wide business approach, as well as being aimed directly at our larger objective to help raise the level of economic opportunity wherever we operate in the world. What we have achieved so far, of course, is only a beginning. I hope that our efforts may continue to bear fruit in the form of a growing base of ownership until the citizens of all the nations and markets of the world which General Motors serves are fully represented.[3]

In the case of General Motors, a corporation which as rapidly as any other is in fact centralising control of world-wide operations, the desire for wider international ownership of GM shares only serves to emphasise that this is primarily a question of overseas public relations, not of industrial reality. This aura of international service, of efficient international co-operation in place of old-fashioned competition, is becoming more and more the self-projected image of much large-scale international industry. While, during the 1970s, the giant international corporations find the answers to these problems of identity, in more and more ways the whole structure and attitude of their management abroad takes on the character of an expanding imperial civil service. The professional literature on the subject of international management echoes the spirit of the British Raj, clothed in the jargon of the business school. Thus, for example, H. C. de Bettignies, an Associate Professor of Organisational Behaviour at INSEAD, and S. H. Rhinesmith, Senior Consultant with the Behavioral Science Center of the Sterling Institute at Cambridge, Massachusetts:

> Over the years, four distinctive patterns of human reaction to new and unfamiliar surroundings have been identified: *"flight"*, *"dependency"*, *"fight"* and *"adjustment"*. When a manager responds to a new situation through *flight*, he rejects the people and the things around him which cause his discomfort and withdraws from any opportunity to interact with them, placing "blame" either on them or on himself for inadequacy in handling the new situation. He reacts defensively, many times fleeing to fellow nationals in a foreign enclave or manifesting other regressive behaviour in order to remove the threatening atmosphere around him and reinstate the security of familiar behavior and beliefs.
>
> Another form of flight is in the opposite direction. In such cases, the manager does not flee from his host culture by joining a foreign enclave, but instead flees from his own national identity by joining the host culture. Such behaviour, often called "going native", is also a means of reducing tension. Accepting this state of *dependency*, such managers lose much of their ability to operate on their own. They attempt to become part of the local culture and in the process lose the perspective necessary for managing an international business enterprise. While such action may be temporarily satisfying to them personally, in the long run the effects of denying one's own cultural identity are many times as harmful personally as they are professionally.*[4]

A company like Du Pont is so concerned about the possibility of good overseas executives "going native" that, after five

---

* The authors conclude that all is not lost and that, with the assistance of management specialists, executives can be prepared for such traumatic experience and taught to use new and unanticipated situations as opportunities for personal growth.

years abroad, it reduces the 20 per cent foreign service premium paid to its American executives by a quarter each year. It does so in order to discourage what it calls "parking in orbit". Other corporations use a good trusted man on several key foreign assignments. This is particularly true of American corporations, which (with the notable exception of IBM) seem to feel happier if they have at least one American crucially placed in their subsidiaries. General Motors is a good example. Between 1928, when GM bought Opel, and 1970, the German car makers had nine Managing Directors. Six of them were Americans. The only exceptions were Fritz von Opel, himself, who remained Managing Director after GM had bought his company, until 1931: a second German, who was appointed when the American Managing Director was obliged to quit in 1941 at the outbreak of hostilities between Germany and the United States: and a third German, who held the fort from the end of the War in 1945 until 1948, when General Motors decided that they would resume full-scale operations in West Germany. Later, in 1970, when General Motors took a further major step in integrating its world-wide activity, three Americans were given overall charge of operations: one in Europe, with a base in England; one for operations in Latin America; and one for operations in Australia, New Zealand, Africa and East Asia. For the European job it chose L. Ralph Mason, at the time its Managing Director at Opel in Germany. GM summarily removed at the same time David Hegland, the Chairman and Managing Director of Vauxhall in the United Kingdom and put in Alexander D. Rhea, until then Managing Director of the successful Australian subsidiary, General Motors Holdens. Rhea's previous career included time with General Motors in Brazil, Venezuela, Germany and in the overseas operations division at New York. He is a good example of the international career executive, who can genuinely claim the widest overseas experience, yet who can still basically be trusted by his head office because he is not a native. The deposed Hegland, himself, had an even more international career for General Motors. Joining the corporation after the War, he served in Sweden,

Belgium, West Germany, Denmark and South Africa, before going to General Motors Holdens in 1961 as Assistant Managing Director, then Managing Director, and moving to head Vauxhall in the United Kingdom in 1966. Du Pont, when it made William B. Hirons Chief Executive of its British operation in 1970, selected a man who came directly from the Du Pont co-ordinating office for Europe in Geneva and who, before that, had been for three years with Du Pont in the Netherlands.

This is the sort of way in which an international corporation can ensure, without elaborate formal structures of control, that its basic philosophy and overall strategy will be understood and implemented. For the senior expatriate manager knows, apart from anything else, that his career prospects depend on the degree to which he serves the interest of the corporation as a whole rather than that of a particular subsidiary.

Traditional methods, like share-incentive schemes designed to link personal wealth to corporate performance, are one popular way of tying individual enthusiasm to the corporation, though in practice they are little more than a way of indirectly increasing some executive salaries. There have, however, been other more radical experiments for increasing managerial commitment to an anonymous corporation. Uniroyal, the American tyre manufacturers, have developed a scheme under which 2 per cent of their graduate intake are identified as potential "fliers" for future top jobs by the time they reach the age of twenty-eight. This 2 per cent is reduced to 1 per cent over the following two years. Then half of these are further weeded out by the age of thirty-two. By that time the graduate recruit will have served in three different countries and in three different Uniroyal divisions. From that $\frac{1}{2}$ per cent of Uniroyal's total graduate intake, all future promotion to top management positions will be made. Unless a Uniroyal executive is so qualified by the age of thirty-two, there is no prospect of his ever reaching the highest levels within the corporation. The corporation has found this to be a system that produces considerable corporate loyalty amongst those who qualify.

In other cases, too, training is used to impart cohesion. As well as founding IMEDE as a schooling ground for its executives, Nestlé has set up a training centre of its own at Vevey, the group's headquarters on the Lake of Geneva. This common strand is a large part of the reason why "Nestlé executives wherever they meet . . . feel an immediate bond not shared by others."[5] IBM has created the same kind of corporate loyalty. Englishmen, Frenchmen and other consider and call themselves IBM-ers.

In the case of Nestlé, the main institutional weapon of central control is its finance department. This is based on a corps of *inspecteurs*, whose task is to travel almost continuously to Nestlé subsidiaries throughout the world to see that accounts are being kept in the way laid down by headquarters at Vevey and that other routine and development procedures obtain equally strict adherence. The theory, which works in practice, is that not much can quickly go wrong, if formal orthodoxy is observed. This then allows the group management at the centre to concentrate its time solely on those areas where things show signs of getting out of line. And Nestlé have other weapons of control. Head office provides a team to supervise the building of new production facilities everywhere; and to monitor the quality of subsequent output, with special concern for trade marks, patents and brand names. All research on new products is centralised and virtually all of it conducted at Vevey. Individual subsidiaries do not communicate with each other, on any but the most informal basis, except through Vevey. Indeed, although the formal structure of the Nestlé empire is loose, there is a strong respect for the centre even in routine public relations, the most local of all activity. A request in writing for quite ordinary information to the British headquarters in a London suburb is liable to get a reply that

Nestlé is an international company, with its headquarters in Vevey in Switzerland and the UK company is just part of this large organisation. The public relations department in the Avenue Nestlé in Vevey would be the people authorised to give out information of this sort.[6]

North American Rockwell, to take another typical example, illustrates the conflict between centralisation in practice and local delegation in theory. It declares that virtually every decision in its subsidiaries is left to local management. However, all policy over new investments, research and development, the introduction of new products and techniques, all financial appropriations and budgets and the vetting of forecasts and reports is a reserved function of the parent company; which somewhat limits the field of local autonomy.

Pirelli, also, before its merger with Dunlop, had centralised all the technical development, design, and manufacturing and engineering development for its tyres and cables in Pirelli, Italy. The various Pirelli subsidiaries all over the world, linked through Pirelli International, are thus under the closest possible control in practice. In this case, all buying of raw materials for the whole of Pirelli's operations outside the European Common Market is centralised in the group office in London. Most important of all, Pirelli has from the start insisted that there should be a small number of high-grade Italian executives from the parent company working in all subsidiaries. In practice Pirelli insists that these reserved posts for Italians should be the Managing Director, or Chief Executive, or perhaps the Finance or the Technical Director. Thus in 1970, at the time of the merger with Dunlop, while the Chairman of Pirelli Ltd in the United Kingdom was Lord Thorneycroft, the Conservative politician and former Chancellor of the Exchequer, its Managing Director was an Italian, Signor Veronesi.*

National governments and national managements both have an instinctive unease about this international centralisation of decision. It was a major part of General de Gaulle's aversion to foreign, particularly American, direct investment in France, that important decisions affecting French interests might be taken outside French control. The findings of one excellent

* When foreign subsidiaries look for local chairmen or honorary presidents of distinction, there is a marked tendency to choose politicians, or those connected with government and the banking community. IBM (UK) chose Lord Cromer, scion of the Baring family and former Governor of the Bank of England, who became British Ambassador at Washington in 1971.

survey of the French complaints was that, while there was little evidence that French national interests were compromised in this way, there was a great deal of evidence that the management of American subsidiaries in France was severely circumscribed in making important and even routine decisions.[7]

The gravamen of the French complaint – that US companies exercise undue control of their subsidiaries – received decided confirmation from the survey. In a significant number of companies, on policy matters touching upon activities vital to the French economy, there was little delegation of authority to subsidiary management.... The centralisation of the decision-making process in the United States appears to be particularly objectionable in view of the offhand manner in which decisions of great consequence abroad are frequently made.[8]

A standard pattern of centralisation, confirmed in this study by Johnstone, is that decisions about finance, such as where, when and how much to borrow, are almost always taken centrally; that this also normally applies to decisions on what sort of machinery should be used for manufacture and whether it should be imported; and that almost invariably policies about dividends and, often, policy on the pricing of products is the preserve of the parent company.

That, at least, is a standard form. It was the direction in which British Ford were pushed when the American parent took full ownership in 1961 and later made it responsible to Ford of Europe. Yet, even then, the form can be different from the reality, as Johnstone showed. His case studies reveal ample examples of central interference, often quoted by an executive who had just declared this to be an area completely reserved for local management.

Thus Johnstone found examples where personnel questions were a local responsibility, except where they touched on budgetary matters. In one of his cases, the practice of serving red wine with meals in the cafeteria of a French subsidiary was reviewed (and happily sustained) by head office in the United States. In another, all labour agreements had to be vetted at head office. One business-machine manufacturer had given clear instructions that trade unions were not to be recognised; a not insignificant limitation on freedom of action in labour relations. One man described the pervasive influence of head office as "the type felt when you know your decision is subject to close review." Johnstone found widespread use of group manuals setting out policy to be followed in a great variety of questions, ranging from the terms of severance pay to the markets in which the subsidiary should sell. Often, Johnstone found, policy was decided by the parent company, without consulting the French subsidiary, which then afterwards had to explain the difficulties caused, or why instructions had not been followed. Often the man responsible for defending the interests of the subsidiary within the group would be an American, with very divided loyalties. Johnstone, who wrote his book on temporary leave of absence from Chrysler International in Switzerland, concluded "that, for at least one-fourth of the subsidiaries, local management enjoyed little autonomy on many issues of vital concern to France."

International corporations have given much thought to the problem of how to maintain high morale in their overseas sub-sidiaries, in the face of the strong trend toward centralisation. This trend is strong even in those international companies that most vehemently preach the gospel of decentralisation.*

ITT is one of a very few major American corporations that have, from time to time, held full board meetings outside the United States, as a gesture; a reminder of the importance of its operations abroad and the fact that its thinking is global. Others include Dow Chemical and IBM, where they make proper play of the fact that the President of IBM World Trade in New York is a Frenchman.

Still other devices have been used to stress this global identity, like taking foreigners on to the main board. Unilever took the president of Lever Brothers (US) on to the parent board; as did

* The Chairman of the British Rio Tinto-Zinc company, Sir Val Duncan, is one of the most convincing advocates of decentralised control. Yet all his overseas subsidiaries are firmly connected by instant telex with London. He will admit that his company's telephone bill is one of the highest in the world and that he, him self, flies some 100,000 miles a year on RTZ business.

the Canadian Massey-Ferguson with the head of their United States subsidiary. In a similar way, four directors went on to the board of American Metal Climax, from Selection Trust, the London mining finance company with a substantial minority holding in the American company.

Yet while this sort of move may help to stress an identity of the parent company with the problems and potentials of its subsidiaries in other countries, it does little to alter the fact that, in the process of integration, local managements are losing their freedom of action, either as nationals of another country, or as managers in their own right. The problem of recruiting a continuing intake of high-quality executives for the future into such a system will be a substantial concern for the international giants over the next twenty years.

5

The Effects

"We have gotten to the stage where a weekend's banking convenience to a single group of banks can create the appearance of a deficit larger than any of the deficits registered in recent years in the struggle of the pound, the French franc, and the lira, not to mention the dollar itself."

JUDD POLK *to the Subcommittee on Foreign Economic Policy of the Joint Economic Committee of the United States Congress, 22 July 1970*

Nationalist reaction to the march of the international leviathan has often been muddled or illogical. When British engineers, working at Hursley in southern England, produce a major model in the IBM 360 computer range, this is taken as further evidence for the superiority of the American corporation; rather than for the high quality of the British educational system that can produce such electronic experts. Yet, when an engineer of Greek parentage and Turkish birth* emigrates to the United Kingdom and there designs cars like the Morris Minor, the Austin-Morris Mini and the Morris 1100, this is taken in some curious way as proof that Britain is not a decadent failure in the world of modern technology. Sentiments of economic nationalism take slow account of changing economic reality.

* Sir Alec Issigonis, who began his career as a draughtsman with Rootes Motors in 1933; became Chief Engineer of the British Motor Corporation; and, after the merger, Technical Director of British Leyland Motor Corporation.

Ordinary trade and finance have been "international" for much longer than manufacturing. They, too, produced autarchic reactions in earlier decades. Thus in 1896, in *The Nineteenth Century*, J. W. Cross felt moved to write:

In the City of London today there is not one single English firm among what might be called the *haute finance*. If a large financial operation has to be concluded we first go to Messrs Rothschild then to Messrs Raphael, both German Jews; then to Messrs S. P. Morgan and Co., an American House; after that, probably to Messrs Speyer or Messrs Seligmann or Messrs Stern, also German Jews; then perhaps to Messrs Hambro, a Danish firm; then to houses like Messrs Fruhling and Goschen, and so on, all foreign houses, and mostly Jews, but there is no strictly English name among them since the unlimited Barings ceased to exist in 1890; and that period during which the Barings' business was best managed was while it was under the direction of Mr Joshua Bates, an American.[1]

Most of those banking houses, whose foreign character concerned Cross in 1896, have survived into the second half of the twentieth century as very *British* institutions. And, to take examples in industry from a small country like Switzerland, there are today no more "Swiss" concerns than Brown, Boveri, the international electrical engineering company, founded by Mr Brown, an Englishman; or Nestlé, the largest Swiss-based company, founded by a German; or Maggi, in soups and foods, founded by an Italian.

Mobility of workers and jobs

Now, however, it is production itself, not just trade and finance that has become international. Consequently, we witness today the same reactions to foreign ownership and control of domestic industry. Politicians and general opinion make considerable play with the assumed need to keep at least key sectors of industry under home ownership. Yet the nation state is crumbling as an economic unit under the impact of international industry. In Switzerland, in 1970, for example, out of an estimated total population of some 6,200,000 and a work force of perhaps 2,800,000, there were no fewer than 900,000 foreign workers. Without them, "Swiss" industry would have ground to a halt. The same is true of West Germany today, where an economic boom is made possible only by the importation of labour from southern Europe, including Yugoslavia. In 1969, the total of these "guest workers" reached 1,400,000.

It is increasingly possible, therefore, to move labour across national boundaries; or to move employment to sources of cheap labour, if that fits better with management's cost and other calculations. This process has seriously qualified our traditional classifications of industry as being Swiss, or Canadian, or Belgian or Dutch. When, during 1969 and 1970, James Schwartzenbach, the independent Swiss deputy, was campaigning for his xenophobic national referendum, designed to expel one third of all foreign workers from Switzerland, Swiss industry made urgent contingency plans for moving over the border into neighbouring parts of France, or for increasing the productive capacity of its existing foreign subsidiaries.

Mass-production, mass-consumption society in industrial countries has provided the framework for this process. To the modern consumer, it is price and quality that matter, not some emotional attachment to "country of manufacture". He does not care whether his colour television set is assembled in the United States, the United Kingdom, Japan or Formosa; whether the Du Pont man-made fibre that goes into his clothes is made in the United States or in Northern Ireland.

There was a time when chauvinist appeals might have had an effect on consumer behaviour. A best-selling book in 1896 could proclaim,

In your own surroundings you will find the material of your own clothes was probably woven in Germany. Still more probable is it that some of your wife's garments are German importations; while it is practically beyond a doubt that the magnificent mantles and jackets wherein her maids array themselves on their Sundays out are German-made and German-sold, for only thus could they be done at the figure. . . .[2]

It continued by stressing the Teutonic origins of items like toys and fairy books for the children; or the Black Forest drinking mug, deceptively inscribed as "a present from Margate". It was supposed that the shock of this realisation would induce the late-nineteenth-century Englishman to pay a premium and Buy British. By 1970, for consumers in any country, there was little of this spirit left.

The new protectionism

The real change is that such sweeping areas of economic and industrial decision have become matters within the discretion of corporate managements; areas like international trade patterns and the distribution of jobs between one country and another. Historically, these questions have been the concern of national governments, whose freedom of action was only tempered by accidents of geography, climate and the chance distribution of natural resources. Today they are increasingly management decisions.

Increasingly, too, international management is encouraging the new wave of protectionism in world trade. This is a complete reversal of a traditional position. For the international giants are finding that they have very distinct interests, which can conflict with the traditional free-trading policies adopted by all major industrial countries for a quarter of a century after the War. In many areas, the managements of international companies have come to see the advantages, in terms of stable planning and reasonable profit, of protected and guaranteed national or regional markets. It is likely that they will do so increasingly during the 1970s and that governments will increasingly make adjustments to their changing requirements.

When we come to look back on the history of the 1970s, it will be seen as the start of a second phase of post-war international economics. The first phase, from 1945 to 1970 was characterised by an irregular but steady progress towards freer trade. The new character of international industry will mean that we shall be moving into a phase when world trade is subject to administrative arrangements settled by negotiation, with international companies as the principals and national governments as the suppliants.

This new mood of protectionism has worked first through those industries which, for physical or psychological reasons, are prevented from "going international". For, until the late 1960s, the major international corporations were in the forefront of the movement for freer world trade. They saw this as the best framework for their continued profitable expansion. It was this philosophy that the father figure of IBM, Thomas Watson Sr, expressed in his slogan "World peace through world trade".

During the later part of the 1960s, however, as the various subsidiaries of international companies became part of the economic and industrial fabric of several nation states, major corporations also became active participants in a new wave of economic protectionism. The old elements of the traditional protectionist lobby have not changed. They consist of governments taking a short-sighted view of their balance of payments and of the need to prop up weaker companies; unable to meet competition from more efficient competitors abroad, especially from those operating in lower wage economies. A new element is the strong switch towards protectionism by organised labour in the United States, made increasingly anxious by the mounting evidence that American corporations, above all in the high-technology industries, are exporting employment to other countries in search of a cheaper work force. Now managements, too, are joining the protectionist camp.

An example is the attitude of the American chemical companies to the proposals for quotas on the import of man-made fibres into the United States. The United States had already curbed imports of steel by means of a "gentleman's agreement", under which Japan and the countries of the Common Market had agreed "voluntarily" to restrict their exports to the United States. This arrangement had all the effect of a formal interference with trade, but avoided the uncomfortable necessity, for the American administration, of formally infringing the principles of free trade.* The Nixon administration during 1970, hoping to head off the more extreme protectionist pressures in Congress, worked for a similar arrangement over man-made fibres, where American domestic industry was particularly concerned about the rising level of imports from Japan, Hong Kong and other countries of the Far East.

At this period, there was one pre-eminent symbol of the American government's will and ability to remain on the path of freer world trade. It was whether the Nixon administration had the political strength to abolish the American Selling Price (ASP). This is a system whereby import duties are levied on a whole range of chemical (benzenoid) products, not on the basis of their import price, but on the much higher price that the same items cost when manufactured in the United States. The purpose of the ASP is straight protection of the domestic chemical industry from cheaper overseas competition. Abolition of the ASP was undertaken in principle by the Johnson administration, as part of the international negotiations at Geneva for lowering tariff barriers in world trade known as the Kennedy Round.†

The United States in fact reneged on this part of the Kennedy Round package. By 1971 there was still no sign that the administration was contemplating the steps necessary to end the ASP system. And the reason was the strongly expressed hostility of the major American chemical corporations, including Du Pont. During 1970, Du Pont and other chemical corporations were prepared to do a political deal with the Nixon administration, in order to get a still greater degree of domestic protection. They indicated that they would be willing to drop their lobbying in favour of retaining the ASP system for benzenoid chemicals, provided that the man-made fibre part of their business was given proper protection from foreign

* As enshrined in the General Agreement on Tariffs and Trade (GATT).

† So called because these international negotiations were undertaken on the initiative of President Kennedy, who asked for and received the necessary powers to negotiate reciprocal agreements with other countries in the 1962 Trade Expansion Act.

imports; either through "voluntary" agreements or through direct American legislation.

There are other industries with the effective political power to demand levels of protection and subsidy that are directly harmful to the interests of the consumer. The most general case is agriculture, where the extreme example is the Common Agricultural Policy of the European Economic Community. But agriculture is a "national" industry. The reason why corporations like Du Pont have modified their policy towards freer international trade is, paradoxically, that they have become so fully international themselves. Once a single corporation, like Du Pont, has established manufacturing capacity in its main markets, it has removed its interest in expanding world trade as such. Then its overwhelming interest is to see that each component of its international group operates in the most profitable climate. It does not even have anything directly to fear from a re-emergence of international trade wars and the imposition of protective tariffs; for it is already well established behind any future protective walls. It sees distinct advantages, in fact, in a series of protected home markets. There is then less possibility of uncomfortable competition from low-cost producers in third countries. Such individual protected markets make it easier to absorb higher labour and other costs, and to plan with confidence for fuller utilisation of capacity, which in capital-intensive industries like chemicals is the critical factor in holding unit costs and protecting profit margins.

The major American corporations in the chemical industry, well established as producers in European and other markets, have therefore curiously turned the wheel full circle. The domestic, American base for their operations has the same interests as a relatively small national company, unconcerned with the export market.

This process of making production international, on the more or less explicit assumption of substantial protection within individual markets, advanced a long way in the motor-car industry as well during the 1960s. It was the basis on which Fiat provided the Soviet Union with technology for the passenger-car manufacturing plant at Togliattigrad. It will be the basis for whatever consortium arrangement emerges for Western automobile groups to build and operate the planned massive truck plant on the Kama River in Northern Russia during the 1970s.*

In the same way, when a country like Nigeria, with a population of some sixty million and the prospect of being the biggest single market for cars in the whole of Africa, decided to establish a car industry, every major international car group in the world put in its bid for the contract. They did so on the assumption that, if successful, they would be producing behind a substantial protective wall, against outside competition from cheaper imports.†

Conflicts of interest

Governments and trade unions alike will have to adjust their attitudes and policies to this changed balance. It is important that they should correctly identify the important aspects of the change and ignore the superficial ones. For, during the 1960s, excessive attention was directed towards the superficial manifestations of international industry. For it was a feature of the decade that, even when the activities of international companies caused a political reaction, it was usually concentrated on the bogus issues connected with national sovereignty. This explains the excessive concentration on such essentially irrelevant issues

* Togliattigrad, named after the Italian Communist Party leader, will be turning out some thirty thousand slightly modified Fiats for the Russian market during the 1970s. Ford showed considerable interest in the proposed truck plant on the Kama River. Modern technology and marketing are no respecters of ideology, and Henry Ford II himself visited Moscow in 1970 for discussions with the Soviet Prime Minister, Alexey Kosygin, and the Minister of Automobile Industry, A. Tarasov. Ford's plans were, however, vetoed by the Nixon administration on political grounds. There followed consideration of whether Ford's foreign subsidiaries, like Ford of Britain, might be able to undertake the task instead, so as to get round the United States embargo.

† In an interesting example of international integration in a world-wide enterprise, the General Motors bid was submitted on behalf of the group by its Australian subsidiary Holdens, because Africa and Australasia are part of the same GM regional group. Neither German Opel, nor British Vauxhall were allowed, by the GM system, to submit bids for the contract in their own right.

as the threat that international corporations might pose to national security.

Here, the classic case was the refusal of the United States government to allow the American computer industry, or its foreign subsidiaries, to supply the French armed forces with large "number crushing" computers during 1963 and 1964, because of the General's uncooperative attitude towards the Western military alliance. And, without these computers, for which there was no native capacity in France, the French independent nuclear defence policy lacked, to be sure, whatever vestige of credibility it might otherwise have had.

For those who consider it possible or desirable for the government of a country the size of France, Germany or the United Kingdom to conduct a nuclear defence strategy on the basis of such total isolation, this limitation may, indeed, present something of a psycho-political problem. It is not, however, easy to sustain a convincing case that during 1963 and 1964 there was, in fact, a sudden dip in the military security of the French Republic. In any case, there are other elements affecting the national interest that enter the equation. A government policy of deliberate support for a first-line computer industry on a national basis inevitably entails giving artificial advantage to second-best national products, at least during the period that the domestic industry is endeavouring to prove its viability. Apart from tax subsidies or helpful rules over "competitive" tendering, this involves real costs. For the "national" computer must either be more expensive or less efficient than the foreign equivalent.* It is a real cost to a bank or other business, if the

* The British Labour Government of 1964–70, for example, introduced the unannounced practice that IBM and other foreign computers had to be 25 per cent cheaper, before they would win contracts over which the government had control. Their Conservative successors continued this general policy, designed to assist the British computer manufacturers, International Computers Ltd. In continental European countries, IBM has a far larger share of each market than in the United Kingdom. There are numerous ways, direct and indirect, in which public-sector contracts of all sorts are steered to national companies. In the Netherlands, Philips are assured of about half the state and other public orders for computers; and Siemens, in practice, enjoy much the same position in West Germany.

performance of a computer is not as good as it could be. It is a real cost to a university research programme, if it cannot get the best possible service for the money it pays.

There is another point in the popular argument about international corporations and national independence. It affects, in general, all high-technology industry, but, again, computers in particular. It is that the computer constitutes the biggest single revolution in post-war industry. Whereas many of today's engineering triumphs, impressive as they may be, are basically extensions of familiar concepts, the capacity of the computer has pushed back all the known boundaries of management and organisation of industry and commerce. It allows the businessman and the industrialist to move into areas of activity previously closed by the limitations of the human mind. Just as in space research and exploration it was the critical development of the computer, rather than of rocketry, that created the possibility of putting men and equipment on to the surface of the moon, so too has the computer become the "commanding height" of the New World's economic and industrial order. This commanding height, the argument goes, should not be left or allowed to pass into foreign control without a struggle. And that struggle may legitimately involve real present sacrifice.

The argument confuses the extensive employment of computers (and the development of computer systems, programmes and other paraphernalia, known collectively as "software") with the design and manufacture of computers themselves, known as the "hardware". There is no evidence that the two are thus connected. There is, for example, no sign that Swiss industry and Swiss international companies, whose operations lend themselves to computer-based control and management techniques, suffer from the fact that there is not – and probably never will be – a Swiss computer industry. There is no evidence, indeed, that American companies enjoy any great advantage in the development of computer "software", despite the dominant American position in making the "hardware". Certainly a whole host of European companies seem able to develop and market computer application systems in the face of any American competition. There is, here, a parellel between the computer and the power station. No-one would claim that it is necessary to be able to design and build an electric power station in order to have a sophisticated electrical or electronics industry. And, on this analogy, it is as yet not necessary to be able to build a computer in order to have a sophisticated information and data-processing industry.

The French anxiety over international corporations was also centred, in the late 1950s and the early 1960s, on several other issues. One was concern that United States companies would not fit co-operatively into the French national system of economic "indicative planning"; that they would be less willing to accept the various suggestions and persuasions of the Commissariat du Plan, the French central planning body which had some prestige at that time. It was a reaction revived in the United Kingdom in 1971 when Chrysler (UK) awarded an 18 per cent wage settlement to its workers at a moment when the government was trying to discourage private-sector industry from conceding high wage settlements.

And there was, above all, the complaint that American companies were buying subsidiaries in France with French money. In one sense this was, and is, indeed true. To take the case of General Motors, in a wider context, the physical value of the corporation's overseas assets in 1950, having recovered its pre-war balance, was something like $180 million;* fifteen years later this figure had multiplied almost six-fold, to $1,100 million. Virtually the whole of this expansion had been financed by funds generated, or borrowed, abroad. American subsidiaries operating in other countries have consistently worked on a high proportion of "debt financing", without having to offer equity shares to those putting up the money. In the United Kingdom, H. J. Heinz, for an initial investment of $200,000, now has an operation earning it more than $2,000,000 a year, built up by ploughing back local profit and raising local money.

In addition, in France in the early 1960s there were several

* Counting working capital and the value of fixed assets, like plant and machinery.

specific incidents that fired industrial xenophobia. In August 1962 General Motors France, then the major French manufacturer of refrigerators, laid off 685 workers out of the 3,100 employed in its plant at Gennevilliers in Paris. The company's excuse was that, with the advantages of the EEC, Italian refrigerators were being imported more cheaply. Within two weeks, Remington Rand (France) announced that it would be laying off 800 of the 1,200 employed in its plant at Caluire-et-Cuire near Lyon, and would move the manufacture of portable typewriters to a more modern plant in the Netherlands. (Eventually, in fact, Remington Rand transferred all its activities from France to the Netherlands and West Germany.) Neither of these substantial redundancy decisions was communicated to the French authorities in advance. And both were seen in France as examples of the way in which the operations of foreign subsidiaries reduce job security. It was alleged that the Remington decision had been taken, without consultation, in the United States and sent by teletype as an order to the subsidiary in France.

The following January Chrysler announced that it had raised its holding in Simca, the French motor-car manufacturer, from 25 per cent to 63·8 per cent, so achieving full control of France's fifth largest company. The operation had been conducted through Swiss banks, with the purchase of Simca shares held outside France. The announcement was made on 18 January 1963, four days after General de Gaulle had vetoed British membership of the EEC, partly at least because of a distaste for Anglo-Saxon economic and industrial influence. On 19 January, the Ministry of Finance called for restriction on outside investment in the EEC. The Finance Minister, M. Valéry Giscard d'Estaing, was reported in the following week to have said, "It is not desirable that important sectors of the Common Market's economy should depend on outside decisions."

Finally, to complete the month, a report appeared in *Le Monde* on 25 January, giving details of a massive $6·5 million canning plant to be built in the Bas-Rhône-Languedoc region by the American company, Libby, McNeill & Libby. The company had been negotiating with the French government for some time and both sides accused the other of being responsible for the press leak. It was the final spark that set off prolonged and widespread concern about national economic integrity.

The immediate casualty of this political deterioration was the negotiations by General Electric to take over the French computer and electronics company, Machines Bull. The French company was in severe financial difficulties and more than willing to let General Electric buy up to 20 per cent of the shares in order to obtain a much needed injection of money and management. The GE application was, however, officially rejected on grounds of higher national policy at the beginning of 1964. There is some irony in the way in which General Electric doggedly persisted with its plans. In mid-1964 it reached agreement on a complex arrangement of holding companies, which gave it effective control of Machines Bull for $43 million, but left an independent company to continue defence work for the French government: GE obtained reluctant French official approval, because it had become clear that there was no other way of saving a major "independent" French computer company. But it then discovered that it could not make the business pay and finally sold out its interest to another American company, Honeywell, in 1970.

All these nationalist objections to the march of the international companies, expressed in most other countries as well during the 1960s*, obscure certain crucial points. In most cases the companies were only taking decisions that national companies in their position would, or should, also have taken. To over-react simply because such particular decisions, with all their unpopular consequences, are being taken by foreign

* One British trade-union leader, Clive Jenkins, reported a conversation with the Managing Director of the British electrical giant GEC-AEI-English Electric, in the course of negotiations about the effects of closing an old plant at Woolwich in London. "You'll have to make up your mind," Arnold (now Sir Arnold) Weinstock is reported to have told Jenkins, "do you want me or the Managing Director of Nippon Electric running the business?" For both men there was an assumed necessity that such a large part of the British electrical industry should be kept out of foreign control.[3]

owners demonstrates a certain lack of perspective and balance in our political and social systems. It is in other more fundamental respects that the international corporations are riding roughshod over the conventions of our national systems.

Trade figures and theory undermined

The most important of these is that the entire basis of traditional trade theory has been undermined, since the distribution of industry around the world is increasingly a managerial decision, taken in the best interests of the corporation as a whole. This issue has two aspects. The first is that, where overseas subsidiaries are a closely integrated part of a single international operation, the flow of components between subsidiaries (in conventional terms, national imports and exports) is no longer directly related to the performance or potential of a national economy.

The extent of this integration is indicated by the following description of General Motors' operations in South Africa:

The Opel components, which in disassembled form are shipped from General Motors plants in West Germany, may reach our Port Elizabeth plant in South Africa for assembly some three and a half weeks later. This is only one shipment from one source. If the South African assembly operation and its recently added manufacturing facilities are to function smoothly and efficiently, they must today receive a carefully controlled and co-ordinated flow of vehicle parts and components from West Germany, England, Canada, the United States and even Australia. These must reach General Motors South Africa in the right volume and at the right time to allow an orderly scheduling of assembly without accumulation of excessive inventories This is a challenging assignment which must be made to work if the investment is to be a profitable one.[4]

The second aspect is that many of the larger international corporations like, for political reasons, to arrange their affairs

* This description also explains why, with modern computing and communication techniques, basic managerial decisions are being increasingly centralised.

so that they produce in particular countries about the equivalent of what they sell there. The whole theory of comparative advantage in international trade is based on the assumption that industry in one country should export increasing amounts of things that it is good at making. This is, therefore, a further major disruption of traditional thinking, caused by the operations of international companies.

Again, it is IBM that has carried this process further than most corporations. It put its position thus in 1970: "IBM's operations, of all kinds, are integrated without regard to national frontiers so as to form a complex of necessary components, hardly any of which would be viable on their own."[5] Thus a typical IBM computer, for example in the 360 range, will be assembled by IBM Deutschland, with IBM components manufactured in and "exported" from France, Italy and the United Kingdom, together with some ancillary equipment made in the United Kingdom, Sweden, Italy and Latin America.

When, with IBM, there is a question of expanding to make a new computer range, the various parts of the IBM empire (in the United Kingdom, France or Germany, for example) compete to get the plum tasks. It is for them a source of pride to be allocated the most challenging missions in an integrated operation. For it is a mark that the corporation as a whole has confidence in the subsidiary's technical and managerial ability. Apart from that, however, the amount of work allocated to each subsidiary will, taking one year with another, be roughly equivalent to the worth of business that the corporation does in each market. When it suited IBM's balance, for example, it moved the manufacture of typewriters from Greenock in Scotland to Amsterdam in the Netherlands. In the same way, the manufacture of a particular computer component, the sorter, was transferred from Scotland to South America. The corporation, like others operating internationally, keeps up-to-date figures for its balance of trade with each country. For it knows that national governments would react to a continuing drain on their balance of trade. An individual government would obviously like IBM's import and export balance to show a positive surplus of trade n its particular national case. But, since IBM must mollify not one but many governments on this score, it has logically decided that minimum overall offence is created if all national IBM accounts are kept in rough export-import balance.

A typical example of this process was the way in which IBM decided in 1970 where the new 370 range of computers was to be built. IBM (UK), the youngest of the major IBM subsidiaries in Europe, was given the "mission" of producing the System 370 Model 165, the biggest computer ever to be manufactured outside the United States. This was taken as confirmation within the corporation that the British subsidiary had "won its spurs" over the years. The next size, the Model 155, was entrusted to the French subsidiary. Yet this change will not mean that the "British" part of IBM will produce a higher level of exports, for the overall production schedules will be adjusted so that imports and exports still remain in rough balance. In the area pre-empted by IBM, there is no longer competition, in the conventional sense, between national computer industries.

This means, however, for a country where IBM is the major computer manufacturer, that there will never be any substantial volume of net exports, no matter how proficient the industry may be. In their capacity as citizens of individual countries, the managers of individual IBM foreign subsidiaries might like and feel able to expand their activities, but have no discretion so to do. It can, for example, be confidently predicted that the next major IBM expansion in Europe will not be by the French, the German or the British subsidiary. It will be the establishment of a new subsidiary in Spain. The reason is not that the Spaniards have shown any particular signs of ability for computer work, nor that the existing subsidiaries in Europe would be unable to expand to cover increased exports to Spain. It is that IBM business, through exports, with Spain is on the point of reaching the level at which relations between the corporation and the Spanish government would be easier if a certain amount of assembly or manufacture were done in Spain. This is particularly critical with products like computers, where the good-will of the government is a major element in securing a large proportion of contracts.

Other corporations are now adopting similar codes of conduct in relation to national governments. ITT, though it is at great pains not to undermine the "national" character of subsidiaries like Standard Telephones and Cables in the United Kingdom, is fully integrated. An ITT subsidiary started manufacturing telephone equipment in Spain as long ago as 1924. Today the flow and interchange of components is complete between its plants in Germany, France, Belgium, Spain, the United Kingdom and even Chile, Brazil and Puerto Rico. Over the years, it has rationalised to the extent that half its output, mainly telephone and related equipment, is manufactured by its European subsidiaries, while the other half of its product range is concentrated in the United States. The advantage to ITT lies in the possibility of substantially longer production runs in individual factories.

The corporation can also balance its imports and exports in individual countries more easily. The Netherlands concern, Philips, is one more example where this sort of integration has advanced rapidly during the 1960s, for the same reasons. During 1968 there was some criticism in the United Kingdom that Philips was running a deficit in its trade with the country as a whole. The position was examined officially by the Industrial Reorganisation Corporation, on behalf of the British Government, and a dinner was arranged in London with Frits Philips himself. Two years later, the concern took some trouble to suggest that matters had been accordingly amended. It would never publicly admit that, in response to the earlier criticism, it had adjusted certain production schedules in favour of the United Kingdom.

An international aircraft like the MRCA* illustrates even more forcibly the way in which international production contradicts conventional balance of trade assumptions. There were official suggestions that joint production of this aircraft for

* See page 39.

European air forces in the 1970s would provide sufficient flexibility to allow a complete offsetting of the foreign exchange costs of keeping British troops stationed in the German Federal Republic, calculated at something like £100 million a year. This could be done simply by re-arranging some of the production schedules so that a greater share of the profit accrued to the United Kingdom. That is a flexibility already possessed by integrated international companies.

Management in the subsidiaries of these integrated international corporations will admit that they are faced with a conflict of interest between overall corporate performance and the national economy, particularly in relation to the national balance of trade and payments. It is a conflict in which they have no choice but to follow the dictates of overall corporate strategy. Their reward is professional pride and increase of status within their corporation.

The national effect is that the path towards higher earnings of foreign exchange through exports is increasingly blocked, as is a higher return on the social and educational costs of providing the work force employed by these subsidiaries. In a national economic sense, it makes no difference whether a trained manager or scientist physically joins the celebrated "brain drain" to the United States, or takes permanent employment with the subsidiary of a United States company. In the areas, therefore, where this international integration has gone furthest – in oil, computers, chemicals or motor vehicles – questions about the trend of imports and exports will become steadily less relevant. An oil company like BP can roughly forecast its net imports of crude oil into the United Kingdom, for they are related to projected demand and BP's share of the British market for petroleum products. But exports will depend not on national considerations, but on managerial decisions about the distribution of the world oil supplies. Whether or not BP exports petroleum products from the United Kingdom will depend solely on whether it can supply a demand more quickly and with greater profit from capacity in the United Kingdom, or from some other source. These decisions already have major effects on published trade statistics; they will increasingly deprive them of real meaning.

Rationalisation in the 1960s, regardless of national boundaries, has been dramatic, too, for a company like Olivetti. While most Olivetti products now sold on the British market are imported, some 80 per cent of the output from British Olivetti's factory at Glasgow in Scotland is exported. In the original Olivetti pattern, the Italian factories made everything. British Olivetti* made office and portable typewriters. Portable typewriters were also made at Barcelona, which was Olivetti's only pre-war foreign investment. Typewriters for the American market were made by its subsidiary Olivetti Underwood, in Connecticut. Rationalisation moved the manufacture of all portable typewriters to Barcelona. The Hartford, Connecticut, plant was closed, and a new one established at Harrisburg, Pennsylvania, with the most modern methods for making electric typewriters and desk-top computers. All manual office-typewriter production was concentrated at Glasgow, which now exports these typewriters to the United States, in place of those previously made by Olivetti Underwood. The output from Scotland, as a result, will have expanded approximately four-fold. A similar reorganisation occurred in the company's nine Italian factories. Each was largely concentrated on making a single Olivetti product, and often one not made at all there in 1967. It is a typical example of the flexibility available to international management.

The effect of managerial discretion on trade flows is also increasingly evident in the motor-car industry, whose export earnings feature large in most national economic plans. Vauxhall, a General Motors subsidiary, no longer attempts to export to the key United States market. Until about 1960, the Vauxhall Victor was exported to the United States with reasonable success. But thereafter the responsibility for the American small-car market within General Motors was given to Opel, though Vauxhall remained the leading "British" make exported to

---

* Founded in 1947; which illustrates how much more quickly the major Italian companies recovered their poise after the War than the Germans.

Canada. Even allowing for the lost export potential of the United States market, there are advantages to this integration from a national point of view. The British subsidiary has the full backing of General Motors' world-wide sales and promotion machinery in other parts of the world. Yet, again, this illustrates the new power of managerial discretion.

So, too, does the Ford decision, announced in August 1970, to build a major $60 million plant, for making automatic gear boxes, at a site just outside Bordeaux in south-west France. Henry Ford II was reported to have been personally involved in this major investment policy. The plant was designed to supply Ford's passenger-car factories in Germany and the United Kingdom, a substantial link in Ford's integrated European operation. The output will feature as French engineering exports. It was not industrially an obvious choice of location. Bordeaux itself is scarcely in the heartland of European industry. Nor is it centrally placed in relation to the rest of Ford's European activity. It had been generally assumed that, on grounds of industrial logic, the plant would be sited near Germany's western border, or perhaps in the Ardennes region, or the Saarland.

The decision was announced, not by Ford, but by M. Chaban-Delmas, Prime Minister of France and simultaneously mayor of Bordeaux, through the local newspaper. The Prime Minister happened to be fighting a difficult by-election campaign at Bordeaux for re-election to the National Assembly, against the exaggerated personality of Jean-Jacques Servan-Schreiber. He made clear political capital out of the decision. It demonstrated to the electors of Bordeaux that he could use the influence of his office to attract modern industry to the town. Ford had decided that the time had come to establish a major plant in France, so as to balance Ford sales in the country. If a rushed determination in favour of Bordeaux would help its relations with the government in a country where all decision-taking is highly centralised, then that, too, was acceptable. Another major industrial decision was thus taken on the basis of managerial discretion, divorced from any notion of a "national" car industry.

An even more significant example of how international corporations are rendering invalid the idea of a national industry is automobile manufacture in Canada. Between 1965 and 1970 the flow of trade between Canada and the United States in this industry was completely reversed. In 1965, when the United States and Canadian governments signed an agreement to remove all tariffs on the import of motor cars or parts in either direction, the balance of trade in "automotive goods" was some $768 million in favour of the United States. Today the Canadian motor-car industry is in effect an extension of the American industry. The major companies, like Ford and General Motors, make no distinction between their domestic and their Canadian operations, either for production or marketing. Production schedules are centrally organised in whatever way best suits technical and managerial requirements. The removal of tariff barriers from 1965 greatly assisted this development. The result, by 1970, was that this Canadian trade deficit had been turned into a surplus, by a net turn-round in under five years worth substantially more than $1,000 million annually. 1970 was a good year from a "Canadian" standpoint, because the American automobile industry happened to have concentrated in Canada the production of what proved to be that year's most popular models. Even for an economy the size of the United States, with its relative indifference to overseas trading accounts, a $1,000 million trading turn-round in one industry is cause for concern. Indeed, it emerged as a major source of friction in 1970 at the high-level meeting of the joint Canadian-United States Committee on Trade and Economic Affairs.

There are myriad other ways, large and small, in which the operations of international companies affect the pattern of trade. For some years, even before there was any question of the full merger announced in 1970, Dunlop did not attempt to export motor vehicle tyres to Italy. It left this market to Pirelli, which manufactured Dunlop tyres under special arrangements. In return, the Dunlop subsidiary in France made Pirelli tyres for the French market. This market-sharing arrangement had the effect of depressing sales of British-made tyres in Italy and Italian-made tyres in France. At that stage the arrangement was between separate companies. Since the merger, as in other large international groups, such market "rationalisation" has been made part of the routine business of management decision.

Even in the food industry, where production and markets are more closely linked because the goods are more perishable, there have been rationalisations that affect trade significantly. Within the European Free Trade Area, Nestlé closed down production facilities in Denmark; and changed to supplying the Danish market from Switzerland.

The conflict between the interests of an international corporation and a national government are often seen most clearly in a developing country. The disagreement during the late 1960s between Shell and the Nigerian government over the exploitation of natural gas is a case in point. Nigeria during the late 1960s was catapulted into the ranks of the world's top ten producers of crude oil. But, for a developing country, oil revenue alone is no guarantee of economic or social development. The Nigerian government was concerned to make use of the natural gas, so often associated with oil wells and flared off as useless in the process of refining crude oil.

The main industrial use of natural gas is as a feedstock for the petrochemical industry. The rise of Nigeria as an oil-producing country has been primarily the work of Shell, which manages a joint Shell-BP exploration company. But Shell and the other international oil companies have been reluctant to establish a Nigerian petrochemical industry. To produce petrochemicals at a reasonable price, the volume of production must be large and the capital investment heavy. The Nigerian market is itself not large enough to justify plant of economic capacity, unless it were to be the basis for a Nigerian export industry. And the international companies have no interest in that prospect, for they already have their petrochemical supply arrangements planned. This leaves only the possibility of smaller, high-cost plants in Nigeria. And, then, the companies would find it cheaper to import from other sources into Nigeria. It is a clear case of the instinctive desire of international companies, where they can, to match production and sales within one country. For the company such policy constitutes rational distribution and use of resources. For the country concerned, it is a severe limit on an independent industrial policy. A country like Nigeria has to accept the benefits that it gets from the world-wide economic and marketing strength of the international oil companies. On its own, it would never have the power in world markets to profit from its own natural resources. At the same time, it has to accept that the wider interests of these international companies may override its own industrial aspirations. Although the issue is thus posed most starkly in the case of a developing country, it is present in the relationship between all nation states and major international corporations.

Migrating Industry

The stage has now been reached where the trading performance of even the United States is affected. About half of the five hundred largest American corporations have substantial manufacturing interests outside the United States. Some forty of them now have more than one-third of their total physical assets abroad. The effect on American trade with the rest of the world has become momentous. In the ten-year period from 1955 to 1964, American exports of finished goods fell by 29 per cent. In the same period, exports of semi-finished goods (mainly the "export" of components and materials to these foreign subsidiaries) rose by 326 per cent.

It is not only the largest corporations that are involved in this process. Willys-Overland, the makers of the original jeep, have twenty-two assembly plants overseas equipped with American-made machinery. Their $70 million of exports a year are largely in the form of components for these plants.

The slow growth of British exports over the years is also significantly due to the fact the British companies are heavily involved in multinational manufacture. The proportionate growth of trade in components between subsidiaries explains the fact that, for example, British exports of motor-car components are now worth more than those of the British motor-car industry itself. It is significant that West Germany, the European country with the most buoyant export performance during the 1960s, is also the country with the least-developed international company sector. Major German companies have concentrated their energy in exporting, rather than in the establishment of foreign subsidiaries.

The American electronics industry is a particularly clear example of how rationalisation by managements has seriously affected both the balance of trade and the level of domestic employment. Between 1966 and 1969, years of rapid expansion for electronic goods, the estimated number of those employed by the industry in the United States fell by over sixty thousand. In those four years, imports of electronic consumer goods (tape-recorders, television sets and the like) rose by something like 300 per cent. In 1960, taking the whole of the electrical and electronic industries, the United States exported 380 per cent, or approaching five times more than it imported.* By 1969 American electrical and electronic exports were a bare 30 per cent higher than imports. And this despite the clear American lead in the application of advanced technology.

Part of this process was increasing competition from Japanese and other industries. But the greatest single factor was the deliberate transfer of technology by American corporations to low-wage countries, where they could produce more profitably for the American and other markets. Indeed, we are fast approaching the point where the United States, the most advanced industrial country in the world, will become a net importer of sophisticated electrical and electronic equipment. This process is different in kind from the normal competition of international trade. For it is happening in science-based, capital-intensive sectors of industry; in the very sectors where American technology has a substantial lead over the rest of the

---

* Figures vary, depending on how the industry is defined.

world. Traditional trading theory would expect that such were just the areas where the United States would exploit its exporting advantage. The reverse is in fact occurring. In the early 1960s, the United States regularly recorded annual trade surpluses of $5,000 million, by which it financed its outflow of capital investment and economic aid. By the end of 1970 American trade with the rest of the world moved into deficit.

This development was the major contributory factor to the 1971 dollar crisis. Without the underpinning of a trade surplus for its other overseas expenditure, the dollar failed to retain its general acceptance as the fulcrum of the post-war monetary system. In this process, American international corporations, in pursuit of their own interests, have played a major role. There are those who argue that, if the United States were free to devalue its currency as others do, it could recover its world competitive position and the balance could be restored. In the present world monetary system, however, the dollar, uniquely, cannot be devalued by unilateral action; for it is the bench-mark for all other currencies. And even when an effective devaluation of the dollar has been engineered (by allowing other currencies to appreciate against the dollar, or by some more fundamental reform of the so-called Bretton Woods monetary system), the amount of such a devaluation required to offset the combined advantages to American corporations of manufacturing in low-wage countries and behind foreign trade barriers, would be quite unacceptable on other grounds. The force of this trend is indicated in that, by 1970, American imports of electronic consumer goods alone had reached a level of about $1,000 million a year; while, between 1962 and 1969, the overall level of American imports grew 50 per cent faster than American exports.

In this process technology has in part, been transferred abroad by traditional licensing. Thus, corporations like General Electric and RCA have granted licences in Japan for a whole range of advanced products, from television components and transistors, through semiconductors, integrated circuits and magnetic memory cores for computers, to mercury and infra-red lamps and optical gun sights.* In part, such licensing agreements have been used as the only practical entry into the highly protected Japanese domestic market. They have, however, also reflected another deliberate attempt at using cheap labour to produce for the American market.

For the same reasons, these American industries are steadily migrating to still lower-wage countries than Japan, in order to continue manufacturing at prices that compete with "Japanese" production. This heavy trend towards establishing wholly-owned subsidiaries in Formosa, Korea, Hong Kong, Singapore and Mexico has implications for employment in the United States that are examined in the following chapter.† It is further accelerated when the low-wage countries themselves, eager for industry, offer generous financial terms to attract it. Thus Formosa offers a five-year holiday, during which foreign companies in certain industries pay no taxes at all, followed by a very low rate of tax, freedom to repatriate profits, a guarantee against nationalisation, and the right to import most materials and machinery free of duty. The Formosa government also offers low-interest loans reaching to 70 per cent of most new plant and even provides some free transport facilities. Singapore, to give another example, exempted certain "pioneer" industries from income tax. These cover the activities in Singapore of corporations like Esso, General Electric, Union Carbide, Gulf Oil and Litton Industries.

* Other American companies in this advanced technology sector, which have entered into licensing agreements of one sort or another with Japanese companies, include Westinghouse, IBM, Sperry Rand, CBS, Bendix, Zenith Radio, Fairchild Camera and Texas Instruments.

† A characteristic of the advanced electronics industry is that, although the technology is sophisticated and the requisite capital equipment expensive, there is also a relatively heavy need for basically unskilled, but dexterous, labour to perform such final functions as assembling, for which machines have not yet been devised. American corporations, with access to both the technology and the capital, see particular advantages for their profitability in moving their manufacture to low-labour-cost areas. Organised labour in the United States was becoming increasingly concerned about this "export" of jobs in the later 1960s. It is the main reason for the swing within the AFL-CIO, away from its traditional policy of supporting free trade, to one of lobbying for protection to maintain the profit margins on American domestic industry.

This search by international companies for the most rational balance between labour and capital costs is not confined to moving high-technology plants to developing countries. The attraction to corporations like IBM of doing extensive research work at integrated centres in Europe (and elsewhere outside the United States) is the saving on salaries and overheads.

To an American motor-car manufacturer like Ford, the attraction of using British and German components, particularly the engine, in its Pinto compact car, manufactured in the United States for the domestic market, was that it seemed to offer a possibility of keeping total costs down below that of its competitors.*

Stateless Money

Rationalisation of physical production across national boundaries has now developed a massive financial counterpart. For the finance departments of industrial corporations are effectively their own international bankers. The effect on national accounts and national monetary and credit systems is already rendering obsolete conventional concepts. The effect will wax rapidly during the 1970s. Already in the monetary upheavals of 1970 and 1971, the authorities in European countries were brought to realise that they had, because of this process, lost control in part of their national monetary systems.

Polk made this point in his Congressional evidence:†

I think we must be close to the point where we should stop worrying about whether companies A, B and C are keeping their funds in a New York bank or its branch in London, or Paris or Frankfurt or

* With a considerable and nationalist fanfare in the British press, Ford of Britain announced, in May 1970, that they had won a multi-million-pound order for making the Pinto engine. Dollar earnings worth £30 – 40 million a year were forecast. An £18 million expansion of engine-making capacity was put in hand at Dagenham in Essex. In the event, because of technical and labour problems, more Pinto engines were initially produced by Ford in West Germany. Within thirteen months, Ford announced that it had changed its plans; European-built Pinto engines would be phased out by 1973, in favour of a new engine plant at Lima, Ohio. Thus ended what had been hailed as potentially "the biggest dollar-earning contract ever held by the *British* motor industry."

† See page 87.

Tokyo; or what the exact national distribution of the companies, equity structure may be. We are close to the point where the meaningful questions, such as whether the companies are in reasonably liquid shape or not, can be faced in dollar terms without making the separate determination in a variety of national currencies.

Already the future capital-investment plans of major corporations are on a scale where the necessary financing will not be available through the savings and the banking system of any one country. The financing requirements of industry, in short, have created a world-wide market for money that does not respect national currencies, or the wishes of national monetary authorities. Indeed, the growth of this international market has been greatly accelerated by the vain efforts of governments (in the first place American, but also British, French and most others) to create national monetary islands to preserve the integrity of domestic economic policy. The bulk of this market is known generically as the Euro-currency market. It consists of a welling pool of money, mainly dollars, in the international banking system, which in one way or another has passed into accounts to which national exchange-control and other regulations do not apply.

The growth of this international money market is unprecedented in modern banking. It is, as always, impossible to get comprehensive and reliable statistics. But, taking the countries of the European Common Market, together with Sweden, Switzerland and the United Kingdom, lending by their banks in dollars went from $9,000 million in 1964 to $47,600 million by the end of 1969. Lending to foreigners in other foreign currencies rose from the equivalent of $3,000 million to $10,200 million in the same period.*

1969 saw the most vigorous expansion of the Euro-currency market. For a combination of reasons, it grew by about 50 per cent in those twelve months. The prolonged credit squeeze in the United States caused American banks to look for dollars else-

* The best estimates for the growth and shape of the Euro-currency markets are contained in the annual reports of the Bank for International Settlements at Basle, Switzerland.[6]

where; and there was heavy borrowing by French and Italian banks, because of respective national exchange-control regulations. On top of this, foreign exchange market operators, private speculators and institutions borrowed dollars in order to buy Deutsche Marks and thus make a profit when the mark was revalued. And, when speculative money flooded out of Germany again after the 1969 revaluation, the German banks themselves were forced to borrow in the Euro-currency market to meet their regular commitments. This picture of the pressures operating during one recent year gives an impression of the way in which the international money market is outside national control and can be used to get round the credit policies of national authorities. But these international funds move through the foreign exchange markets of individual countries. The transactions themselves may only be ledger entries for the dealing banks concerned, but they critically affect the national balance of payments and the state of national reserves.

The Bank for International Settlements (BIS) has estimated that lending in dollars to foreign countries rose by $12,500 million in 1969. Of this total, something like $5,000 million was lent by banks outside the United States to clients outside the United States. Another $500 million lent in this way found its way back, through the Bahamas and some other places, to the United States. The remaining $7,500 million of the 1969 increase was lent back to the United States through American banks.* Some $4,000 million of this sum itself came directly from the United States in the first place, as private American residents and companies moved their money to Europe and other centres, in pursuit of significantly higher interest rates To this extent, in 1969, a substantial slice of the American banking system physically transferred itself outside the United States. The picture as a whole shows how the growth of this fluid international market has created a situation where national money markets are increasingly linked and subject to the same

* BIS estimates are based on official figures from eight European countries. United States statistics showed the foreign borrowing of American banks in 1969 at $9,300 million, higher even than the BIS's $7,500 million.

influences. There is now no way in which a particular country can follow a markedly different credit and interest rate policy from the rest of the industrial world, with the dominant tone being set unilaterally by conditions within the United States. For, if differences of interest rates are significant or prolonged, borrowers and lenders alike can now find ways of accommodating themselves in the international market. Their actions collectively swamp national monetary systems.

It was because of this trend that, during the 1960s, London became again the banking centre of the world. The City had not held such a position since the heyday of British imperial power. With the erosion of British political power and the declining international importance of sterling, the key banking centre for the first half of the twentieth century was New York. One example illustrates the change. In 1922 the London branch of what is now the Morgan Guaranty Trust Company employed over four hundred people. By 1955 this office had been run down to a staff of only just over a hundred. Indeed, the bank did not think it worth rebuilding its office, destroyed by German bombing in 1940, until 1956; and even then it allowed the lease for its site in Lombard Street, a prime site for any bank in the City of London, to lapse because the business did not justify the cost of renewal. In 1956 there were only six American banks with branches in London, all of them established in an earlier era of London's prosperity; and all of them carrying out a very routine and modest line of business.

Fifteen years later, despite deepening problems for the British economy and for sterling, the international revolution had placed the City of London again at the centre of the world financial map. The City of London likes to take a justified professional pride in its financial expertise. But in fact the revolution occurred for four quite external reasons. The first was the American Regulation Q, under which the American authorities place an upper limit on the interest rate that can be paid by domestic banks to attract money on deposit. Banks in the United States were, therefore, limited in their ability to compete for funds in the United States. The second was the

116

American Interest Equalization Tax, designed to protect the American balance of payments by making it financially unattractive for foreigners and foreign companies to borrow money in New York. The third was the United States Department of Commerce Offshore Direct Investment Regulations, which set down limits on the amount of money that American parent companies could take out of the United States for their foreign subsidiaries. (The limits do not apply to Canada.) These also required a certain proportion of profits made abroad to be repatriated to the United States. And the fourth was the United States Federal Reserve's voluntary bank-lending limits, which further restricted the ability of American banks at home to lend to their corporate customers. The result was that a part of the American banking system was forced either to stop business, or leave the country.

The reasons why it chose London for its main evacuation are equally clear. With modern telecommunications, any international bank requires an operations centre in the European time zone. In London, for example, the branch office of an American bank can conduct foreign exchange business with the rest of the world for five or six hours before its New York office comes on the line. And within the European time zone, London has the advantage for Americans that the natives speak English. There is a final, intangible factor. It is the relative attraction of the British way of life, which has for so long drawn in refugees and exiles. One American banker put it thus:

The infrastructure of the UK is also a plus. It is not perfect by any means, but it would be rated superior by world standards, even by US standards. This makes doing business here easier than most other places in the world. I hear constant complaints about the GPO telephones from my British friends, but they have probably never had to struggle with the French telephone system. For those who complain about British Rail, a fitting punishment would be a ride out of New York City on a commuter railroad on an afternoon in August. The comparison can go on and on and generally favourably for the many services which support the City.*

* Daniel P. Davidson of Morgan Guaranty. See page 123.

117

For these reasons there were, by the end of 1970, well over two hundred foreign banks in London. They included the Moscow Narodny Bank and the Bank of China, ranged alongside the representatives of all the leading names in international finance.

This business in stateless money has created an instantaneous world money market, able at a going rate of interest to produce funds in virtually any currency, at virtually any place. The growth of this international banking industry has been the financial reflection of the spread of international industry. For banking is a service. American banks came to Europe during the 1960s, because their most important customers had shown a strong desire to do European and Eurodollar banking business. For the same reasons, British banks have been well up with the leaders in providing an international financing service for companies. In contrast, the great German banks were still, in the 1960s, firmly tied to their home base; because German industry, in general, was relatively slow to develop internationally. Even as late as 1972, not a single German bank had established a branch in London. As more of German industry moves onto an international manufacturing base, with increasingly complex and expanding needs for finance, this introverted posture will change. For, then, even the extensive Frankfurt money market will not, by itself, be sufficient.

A significant development in the growth of a supranational market for money has been the spread of consortium banks. In a way, the lead was given in 1964 by the Midland Bank in the United Kingdom, when it took the initiative in establishing the Midland and International Bank Ltd (MAIBL) in partnership with the Commercial Bank of Australia, Standard Bank and Toronto Dominion. But this pioneer venture was, and still largely is, confined to meeting loan requirements of corporations within the sterling area. The growth area for international finance is now in dollars and other non-sterling currencies. By the end of 1970, there were over a dozen such consortia based in London alone.

Typical is the Orion group established in London in 1970. While some of the earlier consortia were loose federations of independent national banks, with advantages based mainly on mutual support, Orion could be the model for a more integrated international operation. The first partners in Orion were each already themselves ranked amongst the world's twenty largest banks. They were the Chase Manhattan in New York, the National Westminster Bank in London, the Royal Bank of Canada and the Westdeutsche Landesbank Girozentrale, a Frankfurt savings institution and the bank with the largest deposits in Germany. The avowed aim of the group was to provide complete financial services of the sort required by international companies; through an international merchant bank, Orion Bank, and through Orion Termbank, specialising in medium-term loans. All except the German bank, which is a relative newcomer to international finance, already had extensive international networks. National Westminster, for example, already had a major interest in the International Commercial Bank, set up in 1967, with the Irving Trust in New York, the First National Bank of Chicago, the Hong Kong and Shanghai Bank in the Far East and the Commerzbank in Germany. Orion, however, is an implicit admission that the financing requirements of international industry are now so large that they cannot be met by any one bank, no matter how good its network of branches and arrangements around the world. Even by 1970, banks operating in this international medium-term loan market, mainly for international industry, were being asked to find between $2,000 million and $3,000 million a year. The trend is certain to continue sharply upwards during the 1970s.

The international message had fully penetrated even the traditionally insular world of French banking by the late 1960s. The French merchant banks, like Lazard Frères, the Banque Rothschild and Suez have been making an increasing impact on this international stage. The great French commercial banks were slower to move. But, even here, Crédit Lyonnais arranged a virtual merger with the German Commerzbank in 1970.*

* It could not be a full merger because, in common with the other French commercial banks, Crédit Lyonnais is a nationalised concern. In every other way, the link seems intended to be as close as if the two banks had merged.

119

A similar example was European Financial Associates, incorporated in the Netherlands in 1970, with its first office in London. Such an arrangement allowed the new group the convenience of operating in the world's main money market, coupled with the flexibility of being legally based outside the United Kingdom. The partners in this case were drawn from the European banking establishment. They were the Amsterdam-Rotterdam Bank and Pierson, Heldring and Pierson, both in Amsterdam; the Deutsche Bank in Frankfurt; N. M. Rothschild in London; and the ubiquitous Société Générale de Banque in Brussels. Again the avowed purpose was to provide an international network capable of providing the transnational services required by the international corporation.

The consortia derive their potential flexibility from the ability to circumvent specific national problems and restrictions. Thus American banks can do a range of foreign investment banking, closed to them by domestic regulations when operating from their home base. British and French banks are offered the opportunity to do business outside the stringent restrictions of their respective exchange-control . and credit regulations. Netherlands banks operating in this way can do so, free from the domestic limits on their freedom to deploy their assets.

The significance of these developments for the world monetary system can scarcely be exaggerated. There are those who resent such a major breach in national control over monetary and economic policy. Thus M. Valéry Giscard d'Estaing, the French Minister of Economics and Finance, told the 1970 annual meeting of the International Monetary Fund at Copenhagen that his government would wish to be associated with any common effort to bring order to the Eurodollar market; "to bring order to a situation which shows the obvious paradox of a universal effort to improve [national] credit policy and the total absence of organisation and supervision of this market." He knew, as the French minister responsible, how France (and other countries like the United Kingdom and Italy) had suffered from the surges in this reservoir of international money during the steady succession of currency crises from 1967 to 1969. No

French or other national exchange-control regulations, no matter how comprehensive and diligently applied, can for long do anything substantial to contain such movements of money.

By the late 1960s, there was increasing concern over the irresponsible nature of this new international money market. Massive sums of money were being circulated, without the basis of those rules, regulations or conventions that national governments and banking systems have come to consider prudent, over decades and centuries, in the wake of spectacular scandals and banking failures. For the more cautious members of the banking fraternity, the fundamental worry is the constant violation of banking's first precept, "Do not borrow short and lend long." In this Euro-currency market, most of the money placed with the banks is on a day-to-day basis, or at best for one, three, six or twelve months. At the same time much of the lending by the banks themselves goes into long and medium-term commitments. The result is a dangerously unstable pyramid, where one major failure could leave a domino trail of operators, with immediate money to find and all their resources lent out for long periods.

For this reason, rather than out of concern for the integrity of national economic and monetary policies, bankers operating in this market were, by 1970, themselves discussing the need for supranational regulation; for some collective action by governments to establish ground rules for a market that had long since become international. The problem remains, however, of how to regulate this market, while not at the same time destroying its qualities of international flexibility. Its success in meeting the expanding needs of international industry, where national banking systems have become too small, is the justification for its continued existence. National governments thus remain ambivalent. For, since the War, they have deliberately and painstakingly co-operated to create the open investment and banking system responsible. They did so in the belief that this was the best framework for growing economic prosperity; a belief stemming from their experiences of economic nationalism in the inter-war period. But, when faced with the consequences of that freedom, these same national governments react with suspicion and hostility.

At times when currency speculation has caused the maximum difficulty for national governments, politicians have projected the idea that responsibility lay with wicked speculators. It was the habit of Harold Wilson, during the sterling crises of the mid-1960s, to pretend that international speculators were conspiring to undermine British progress towards his particular vision of a fair society. He gave currency to the label "the Gnomes of Zurich" for this malign group of foreign subversives.

In 1971, President Nixon also considered that similar sentiments would go down well with his own electorate. Announcing his package of measures to help the American domestic economy and the dollar abroad, he said,

> In the past seven years, there has been an average of one international monetary crisis every year. Who gains from these crises? Not the working man, not the investor, not the real producers of wealth. The gainers are the international money speculators. Because they thrive on crises, they help to create them.
>
> In recent weeks the speculators have been waging an all-out war on the American dollar. . . . Accordingly, I have directed the Secretary of the Treasury to take the action necessary to defend the dollar against the speculators. . . .
>
> This action will not win us any friends among the international money traders. But our primary concern is with the American workers, and with fair competition round the world.[7]

Bretton Woods system destroyed

There certainly are speculators, in the strict sense; but their influence is peripheral. It is the legitimate operations of international companies (and the banks that serve them) that brought the post-war monetary system to its knees in 1971. For the system established at Bretton Woods, New Hampshire, in 1944 was based on fixed exchange rates, which only altered under extreme circumstances. This relative rigidity of the structure was quite unable to stand up against the tidal waves of money that international business had generated by 1970.

122

There is nothing speculative or immoral in what was occurring. International corporations may at any given moment have an overall balance sheet in a dozen or more currencies. This gives them both the commercial *need* and the commercial *means* to protect their interests by "speculating", or (more politely) "taking positions" in the foreign-exchange markets.

One American banker put it thus in 1970, with particular reference to British experience,

> During the sterling crises of the past several years, there have been mutterings about bringing the speculators against sterling to heel. These speculators are sometimes mysteriously referred to as the gnomes of Zurich. Well, the Bank of England knows . . . that the bear raids against sterling have largely been mounted through use of the Euro-market and the operators in that market are not necessarily resident in the Alps.
>
> There have been a number of angry cries, from the Continent particularly, about the mindless beast that tramples on the currencies of the world. The Euro-market has repeatedly tilted domestic economies in directions they were not supposed to go. This upsets the hoped-for order of central bankers, it often infuriates their political bosses. Those of us who have substantial positions in the Euro-market are concerned about the possibilities of international regulation.[8]

There was a similar reaction from the American business community to President Nixon's populist analysis of the 1971 dollar crisis. Typical was a story carried in the *Wall Street Journal* from Englewood Cliffs, New Jersey:

> President Nixon is blaming the weakness of the dollar in world markets, in large part, on international money speculators.
>
> Well, it appears a nest of these rascals is in operation right here on the Hudson River Palisades. The Gnomes of New Jersey, it seems are busily engaged in bollixing up world financial structures with such weapons as Hellmann's mayonnaise, Skippy peanut butter, Bosco and Shinola.
>
> This is the headquarters, right out in the open, of **CPC International Inc.**, the 82nd largest industrial company in the US and a major multinational manufacturer and distributor of food and industrial products. CPC (It used to be Corn Products Refining Co.) has

operations in 39 nations; of its 44,000 employees, 25,000 are abroad. And it does business in dozens of currencies. In the course of a year, CPC engages in monetary transactions across national borders amounting to many millions of dollars, marks, francs, yen, pesos, cruzeiros, baht and kip.[9]

The article continued with a typical description of the ways in which a corporation like CPC contributes to monetary instability, through the proper exercise of its commercial functions. Such instability comes with the acceleration of payments, where these are due in strong currencies, which might revalue, or float upwards, in the foreign-exchange markets; and with the reverse lagging of payments, which require to be paid in weak currencies. There is, also, the lengthening of credit in hard-currency countries and the stockpiling of, in CPC's case, commodities and raw material in countries where a devaluation is imminent. All these activities will work precisely in the direction of further strengthening those currencies which have been generally identified as strong, and weakening those that are suspect.

More and more companies have departments whose sole function is to "take views" about the future performance of currencies and to adjust their corporation's stock buying, investment and credit positions accordingly.* Some companies have taken this to the stage where they construct their own system of exchange rates for currencies, designed to reflect more subjective judgements about the future profits in each particular country. They would then apply this rate internally when making decisions about future overall corporate strategy.

Since the experts usually come to similar conclusions about the strength of a currency, there developed a Gadarene instability that, in 1971, finally broke the fixed exchange-rate system. Whatever monetary order survives for the remainder of this century, it will be significantly different from the one that has worked, with relative smoothness, since the end of the Second

---

* *Fortune* (15 September 1969) claimed that almost all American parent companies had instructed their British subsidiaries, before the 1967 sterling devaluation, to arrange payments so that as little money as possible was held in pounds.

124

World War. The finance departments of international corporations have made sure of that. Even the most patriotic company, subject to the closest scrutiny by the guardians of national exchange-control regulations, ceases to press its subsidiaries to settle accounts, and hastens somewhat to settle its own, in order to minimise the effects of, say, an impending devaluation. With the British devaluation of November 1967, the substantial majority of international companies operating in the United Kingdom had fully covered themselves in advance by establishing positions in the forward currency markets.*

This new instability, as national governments consider it, arising from the international integration of finance, has been recognised and described for what it is by Paul Volcker, the Under Secretary responsible for monetary affairs in the United States Treasury and the intellectual force behind the Nixon administration's thinking on these issues:

> Recent experience is replete with examples of massive capital flows across national borders, sometimes for speculative reasons, but also in response to normal market incentives. The reasons are fundamental. National financial markets have grown both larger and more integrated. . . .
> Indeed it is at least as easy – and probably substantially easier – for a New York bank to deal with its branch or correspondent in London today than it would have been for the same bank to deal with its Chicago or St Louis correspondent twenty years ago. . . .
> The growth in the number of US banks with offices in Brussels is one reflection of a world-wide phenomenon. The number of branches and subsidiaries throughout the world of such foreign banks has reached some four hundred – quadrupling in the past fifteen years. There are about a hundred offices of foreign banks in the United States. The rise of multinational corporations, with vast amounts of liquid funds at their disposal and close banking contacts in a variety of key markets, is another dimension. . . . Large and closely-integrated markets mean that funds will move quickly and react in

---

* The process is simply one of buying or selling foreign currency at a rate quoted today, but for delivery one, three, six or twelve months in advance; thus leapfrogging any intervening exchange-rate charge and providing short-term certainty for traders and others.

volume to relatively small incentives. Sometimes these international shifts will help support domestic or balance of payments objectives; but they will often appear to be working at cross-purposes with national policies. Thus questions are posed, both for the independence of national policies and for the international monetary system.[10]

There has, in the past, been a conspiracy to obscure these trends. Politicians in government have been conspirators, because they have been professionally reluctant to recognise or advertise the degree to which they are not in control of their own economic environment. Theirs is the ungainly posture of responsibility without power. International bankers and industrialists, too, have been party to the conspiracy; because in their own self-interest they do not wish attention to be drawn to the fact that their powers are growing at the expense of governments in fundamental questions of national economic policy.

Such a conspiracy in the matter of public relations, however, does not change the reality, about which politicians, bankers and industrialists are, at last, beginning to talk more freely. This reality was expressed by Walter H. Page, Vice-Chairman of Morgan Guaranty Trust Company in 1969. "It is time that governments show greater confidence in the viability of the international financial structure, and greater willingness to make needed reforms in their domestic economies rather than abridge that free flow of trade and investment. . . . There is a fundamental futility in all attempts to seal markets and moneys off from each other."[11] Page is here clearly stating that governments must cut their coat to the cloth of international business.

It was, in the first place, the major oil companies that created this world of finance on a scale where it critically affected the reserves of even a major central bank, like the Bank of England. As an oil-company treasurer is reputed to have said, "When I write a cheque, it is the bank that bounces." The British case is particularly striking, because the United Kingdom is the base for both British Petroleum and the Anglo-Dutch Shell group. But this is only a question of degree. In most oil-producing

126

countries, the cash generated by the industry constitutes the greater part of their monetary system and of their foreign-exchange transactions.

The impact of the oil industry is, however, also substantial in industrial countries. In Germany, for example, a single subsidiary, Deutsche Shell, wholly-owned by the Shell group, may have to find some DM 2,500 million for planned expansion of its facilities, particularly in the petrochemical field, between 1970 and 1975. This finance will, in the main, have to be produced locally since, in the Shell group as a whole, there will be equivalent demands for money made by subsidiaries in other countries. And Shell in Germany is only one small part of the huge demand for finance building up from international business in the 1970s. Already, those responsible for finance in the oil industry are saying in private that the whole Euro-currency market will not be sufficient for their own planned requirements. This uncontrolled pressure for more money and resources is likely to be one of the strongest forces fueling inflation, rising prices and higher interest rates in the 1970s. National governments will have to live with the consequences, economic and social. They are losing the power to influence the outcome.

In the British case, the requirements of the oil companies are so large that there is regular close consultation with the Treasury. The practice has been established where the major British-based oil companies submit a quarterly statement of their spending requirements, together with the ways in which it is proposed to find the financing. The purpose is not to enable the authorities to interfere, but to give them warning of the possible effects on the British reserves, so that they can make appropriate dispositions. The Treasury have occasionally asked for temporary cut-backs or postponements, when an uncomfortably large requirement for sterling in a particular quarterly period might cause difficulties. But, in general, the oil companies have been given concessionary treatment in the exchange-control regulations, in recognition of the fact that they are operating in an internationally integrated world environment. There is no instance in which the consultations with the British Treasury have materially affected planned expenditure by these oil companies. In the case of Shell, the British authorities know full well that substantial interference in this way would result in the group moving its commercial centre of gravity to the Netherlands.

It is BP's size and international character that determine the special relationship of the company with the British government. It has little or nothing to do with the fact that the government has owned half of the company since 1914, when Winston Churchill, as First Lord of the Admiralty, sought to ensure in this way a British supplier of oil for the Royal Navy, which was switching from coal as its basic fuel.

In principle, a company like BP keeps all its liquid finds in London; though subsidiaries the size, for example, of BP Deutschland, have to keep substantial working balances about the globe, sometimes to meet local legal requirements, more often out of operational caution. In the case of virtually all companies operating internationally, the control of money and borrowing is highly centralised. In the case of the oil companies, the scale of operations is such that an uncoordinated move by a major subsidiary could affect the international money market as a whole. This applied particularly in the 1960s to borrowing on the open Swiss and German money markets and to Euro-currency. The same is true for any international group requiring money on a similar scale. Part of the reason for this close control is that an international group has to watch carefully its global debt position, long- or short-term in relation to its revenue.

This centrally directed finance, cumulatively, results in abrupt movement of funds about the world, greatly exceeding the value of any real economic or industrial activity. The effects of commercial lending, borrowing, and dividend or profit policy, in short, are becoming increasingly dominant factors in the framework of national balance sheets. The operational flexibility and cohesion of the international company is just beginning to be recognised in official statements about international payments and reserves. These have begun to contain phrases like, "The most important factor leading to the rise in the net receipts of interest, profits and dividends is a very large rise in the net receipts of UK oil companies"; or, "Outward direct investment was again well up on the previous year, a large part of the increase being over inter-company accounts."[12] In explaining a £22 million inflow of funds for private investments into the United Kingdom between January and March 1970, a major part was estimated to be "a very substantial movement of funds into the UK over inter-company accounts, particularly in the form of import credit from foreign parent companies."[13] The reason for this inflow was that international companies were able to protect their subsidiaries in the United Kingdom, or use their subsidiaries abroad, to offset the effects of the prolonged British credit squeeze. Companies will become increasingly sophisticated about ways in which they can get round national attempts to use exchange control and instruments of credit policy for "national" economic ends. The September 1970 report from the Federal Reserve Bank of New York also commented, ". . . during the first four months of 1970 . . . London began to attract very heavy inflows of short-term investment funds. . . . In addition, British-based firms with international subsidiaries apparently were bringing funds home to bolster their liquidity positions." If the incentives, or the difficulties, are significant, international companies can and do react to them by adjusting the flow of cash involved in their operations.

The absolute figures for the impact on the United States are even more striking. It is estimated that a net $6,000 million was moved into the United States during 1969 alone, in the form of liquid capital in the hands of international companies and banks. In relation to the size of the domestic American economy, such figures take on a somewhat reduced perspective. But to the other industrial countries of the world, the effect is of a great monetary tidal wave, surging and ebbing about the world; a volume of money required by international industry, answering only to the impersonal international forces of interest. And the flow of ordinary profits remitted from operations abroad is even a major factor in the American balance of payments.* The dividend policy of American subsidiaries has also become a major factor in the balance of payments of other industrial countries. Since 1963 American subsidiaries in the United Kingdom have remitted between 53 and 59 per cent of their profits to the United States.†

This proportion for the United Kingdom is low in comparison with the practice of American corporations in Europe as a whole. For the countries of the present European Economic Community, remittances have averaged over 80 per cent of profits in recent years. In 1965 this figure went as high as 93 per cent. If this EEC average were the practice in the United Kingdom, it would represent an extra drain on the British reserves of some £300 million a year. In general, for the industrial countries of Europe, there was a clear pattern during the 1950s and early 1960s for American subsidiaries to plough back 50 to 60 per cent of their operating profits in further expansion. Since the mid-1960s, the strong trend has been towards higher remittances, thus strengthening the "invisible" earnings in the American current account. In particular countries, the process has gone even further. American subsidiaries in Sweden have taken more than 100 per cent of their earnings out of the country every year since 1958, with the exceptions of 1963 and 1964. In 1968 this figure touched almost 160 per cent of earnings, as American subsidiaries repatriated nearly 60 per cent more than the profits they earned in Sweden that year. In Spain, where the post-war expansion of American industry came later

* The figure for the profits of British subsidiaries, made overseas and brought back to the United Kingdom, rose over 200 per cent in the 1960s, to a figure of more than £300 million in 1969, with the trend still rising sharply.

† The single exception was 1967 (the year when, in November, sterling was devalued against the dollar) when the figure leaped to 73 per cent. The calculation takes total dividends and interest payments, net of any withholding taxes, credited to a subsidiary's American owner; together with profits of branches, net of foreign taxes, but before American taxes. These are then expressed as a percentage of the United States share of net earnings, or losses, of foreign companies and branches; again net of foreign, but before American, taxes. The estimates are published periodically by the United States Department of Commerce in its *Survey of Current Business*.

than elsewhere in Europe, all profits were ploughed back between about 1956 and 1960. But, by the end of the 1960s, American subsidiaries were taking out about 90 per cent of their operating profits. In 1965 American subsidiaries repatriated from Italy thirty-two times as much as they made in total earnings, by running down their cash holdings in the country and by taking money out of subsidiaries that were showing little profit (or even a loss). In Denmark the proportion repatriated was eight and ten times total earnings in 1967 and 1968 respectively.

Analysed by industry, the change in the 1960s was most marked in petroleum. American oil companies, having built up their stake in Europe in the 1950s and early 1960s, began to repatriate substantially more than they were earning, at least as shown in the accounts, from about the mid-1960s. The figure was nine times as much in 1964, twenty times as much in 1966, thirty-five times as much in 1968.

By the end of the 1960s, American industry was bringing home an estimated $8,000 million a year in interest, profit and dividends from its operations in other countries. That figure is a measure of the degree to which American industry was organised on lines that disregarded the boundaries of nation states. The continuing profitability in 1970 of a corporation like IBM, for instance, was dependent almost wholly on the growth of its profits in Europe. In one year, 1969, one corporation, General Motors, contributed $465 million to the American balance of payments figures from the remitted profits on its operations outside the United States. Between 1945 and 1969, GM contributed no less than $12,800 million in this way.

There are also single acts of company policy on such a scale that they affect the payments and reserves of countries the size of the United Kingdom. Thus the new royalty and tax arrangements between the major oil companies and the oil-producing countries of the Persian Gulf in the early spring of 1971 will be an extra burden of at least £100 million each year on the British balance of payments, an annual sum equivalent to not far from a tenth of the entire gold and convertible currency reserves of the Bank of England. Even at an earlier period, when the American corporation Ford bought out the minority share-holding in Ford in the United Kingdom in 1961 for £130 million, the sum involved was a major factor for the British balance of payments and the condition of the official reserves. Indeed, in the difficult period for sterling between 1967 and 1969, it was more than once said, and only half in jest, that the situation was hopeless, unless some American company came up with a good cash takeover bid for a British company.

And there have been variations of policy on profit repatria-tion even between American corporations in the same industry. Ford, for example, has followed a general policy of financing expansion out of retained earnings. General Motors, in contrast, has normally repatriated a much higher proportion of its earnings. For its major expansion plan at Antwerp, General Motors went to the European capital market for $100 million of new money.

This example raises a further aspect of international corpor-ate finance. For General Motors was able to get that money on extremely favourable terms.* The unquestioned advantages that American corporations seemed to have during the 1960s have been somewhat dissipated. Major financial crashes, such as those of Allied Crude Vegetable Oil and the Penn Central railroad, brought home to the European financial community that a loan was not automatically safe just because the borrower was large and American. There is, at last, the beginning of more realistic investigation of credit-worthiness. But the psychological advantage that the large American-based corporations have when they wish to raise money in European and international money markets is likely to remain substantial. In part, this applies also to any established company with a proven inter-national record.

Much of the reason for this lies in the undevelop╌d nature of the capital markets of continental Europe. Unlike the situation

---

* Half the money was put up at between 2 and $2\frac{1}{2}$ per cent under the going market rates by the government-sponsored Société Nationale de Crédit à l'Indus-trie.

in parts of the United States, there is a marked lack of institutional machinery for putting up genuinely "risk" capital. In the United States it is relatively easy for a single entrepreneur, or group, with a new and feasible industrial project, to find sources of finance. This element of "gambling", with high returns for the investor when an idea succeeds and high rates of total failure, is not a feature of the European banking and investing scene. Security of investment is much more widely prized. Since there is a link between size and security (even if there is none between size and profitability) and since American corporations dominate the list of the world's largest companies, these have a built-in advantage when raising finance in Europe.

The other part of the explanation lies in the equally undeveloped state of European company law. American and British companies are required to make public a measure of information about their financial activities that is unknown in continental Europe. A consequence, for example, of the merger between Dunlop and Pirelli in 1970 was that, for the first time, a major Italian company had to make a relatively full disclosure of its financial position; so that the terms of the merger could be properly put to the Dunlop shareholders.

The general secrecy of company finance on the Continent is a major factor in the reluctance of the general financial community at large to advance money to European companies in the free way that it is advanced to American, and to a lesser extent British, companies. It is also the reason why the stock exchanges of continental Europe are such limited affairs, compared with those of London and New York. Even in the American and British cases there have been periodic scandals, because the investing public has been misled over the affairs of a particular company. In the majority of continental countries, however, the investing public has not the beginnings of sufficient information to reach rational investment decisions. In these respects American and British companies operate in a framework of law and public opinion that is fully forty years in advance of practice in continental Europe. The result is that

European investors instinctively put more trust in established American, British and international companies.

In particular countries, like Spain and Italy, it is acknowledged quite openly that published trading and profit figures bear no relation to reality. One study of Spanish business[14] reported a Spanish manager as saying that his company and all others in his industry under-reported their production figures in order to cut their tax bill. His proof was that Spanish official figures for his industry, based on company returns, put the total output at only 20 per cent more than the true output of his company alone, while he was certain that at least five other companies had true outputs larger than his own. Most international companies operating in Spain have come to terms with this sort of local business practice and ethic. It is, meanwhile, an illustration of the reason why international companies, where at least the parent company's balance sheet and accounts are published in some detail, find it easier to attract money.

In part to exploit this financial strength and flexibility, in part to minimise overall tax liability, the international company has taken the lead in developing the holding company as part of its integrated organisation. Company law in different countries provides particular advantages for particular types of operation. In the popular imagination, the tax-havens of the Caribbean, or of small European principalities, feature large. In fact, holding companies in the Netherlands, Luxembourg, Canada or Switzerland offer comparable benefits for particular kinds of business. Tax minimisation apart, the advantage for the international company is more in the area of centralised financial control. It is easier and cheaper for Standard Oil of New Jersey to channel its European financing operations through its holding company in Luxembourg. Du Pont does its financial co-ordination through its European office at Geneva in Switzerland. The existence of such holding companies is sufficiently extensive in the case of Switzerland, Canada and Panama to distort significantly the official figures for international investment flows. Estimates for investment in other countries from these three sources include a substantial volume that is in fact the activity of an international holding company, operating from such a base for some tactical reason.

The main advantage of the holding-company technique is that it can be used to delay the final payment of taxes by the parent company. In specific cases, it is certainly also possible to avoid taxation; but most of the significant international companies are under such constant and suspicious surveillance by their national tax authorities that this is not likely, in their case, to be extensive. By channelling profits through a holding company in a third country, however, it is possible to introduce a substantial time-lag between making a profit and the final payment of tax on it. And tax payment delayed is money saved, particularly with world interest rates as high as they have been during the late 1960s. The holding-company technique also makes it easier to set losses against profits to reduce tax liability.

It is not only American corporations that have exploited the holding-company technique. Pirelli has used a Swiss holding company at Basle since shortly after the First World War. Pirelli International, the hub of Pirelli's network outside the EEC, is a Swiss company. After 1918 Pirelli wanted the advantages of running its foreign financial affairs from within the framework of Swiss law and Swiss banking secrecy, instead of from Italy. It gave Pirelli the added advantage, for example during the Second World War, that its subsidiaries in other countries were legally owned by a parent company in a neutral country. And, as a Swiss company it had easier access to the Swiss money markets. There was no formal Pirelli ownership, even, of Pirelli International. The only connection of that sort was the reverse, with Pirelli International at Basle owning a 12 per cent minority holding in the Italian company, Pirelli SpA. But the Swiss holding company was, in fact, linked on a personal and technical level, just as closely as if it had been a wholly-owned subsidiary. There was a formal assistance agreement between Pirelli International and Pirelli SpA, which ensured that all technical development was carried out in Italy. For this,

Pirelli in Italy gets substantial payments from its subsidiaries; not in the form of dividends, but as payments for technical assistance. These technical links also ensure that the policy control is total.*

Even French companies, in general the slowest to become international in outlook and operation, have used the foreign holding company extensively. Michelin has its international headquarters at Basle in Switzerland. St Gobain, the glass-makers, have their operations centred at Fribourg in Switzerland. Renault, the government-owned car makers, have a Swiss holding company for some operations. So, too, do the Italian companies Olivetti and Montedison; the Belgian chemical company, Solvay; and the German chemical companies, BASF and Bayer. Olivetti also set up a Luxembourg holding company in 1961 to co-ordinate its international funding.

International corporations, in short, must now actively speculate (or take positions, to use an emotionally neutral term) in national currencies. B. A. Lietaer has worked out a model which corporation treasurers could use as the basis for a computer programme to assess the risk that they carry at any given moment from possible currency revaluations or devaluations.[15] He has developed a concept of "net exposure"; the balance of liabilities in other currencies that would be affected by exchange-rate changes anywhere in the world. This sort of approach is increasingly influencing corporate finance directors, for their professional reputation depends upon not getting caught.

There were some substantial losses and gains, for example, as a result of the British devaluation in November 1967, and the other exchange-rate changes that went with it. Thus the Hoover Corporation lost the equivalent of $6·9 million as a result of 1967 devaluations in the United Kingdom, Finland and Denmark. This loss represented 55 cents per Hoover share, in a year when total earnings were worth $2·09 per share.

* The ownership structure of Pirelli and its subsidiaries was substantially changed from 1 January 1971, because of the merger with the world-wide interests of Dunlop.

Eastman-Kodak estimated its total loss as a result of the 1967 devaluations at $9·5 million, of which some $8 million was due to the British devaluation alone. The company lost a further $2·5 million because of devaluations in 1968. International Telephone and Telegraph reported a small loss of $3·2 million, despite vigorous attempts to protect themselves by operating in the foreign-exchange markets. Firestone reported a loss from devaluations in 1966 of $4·2 million, and in 1967 of $6·5 million.

Ensuring that losses from a devaluation will be matched by profits from currency dealings can be expensive, especially when the "insurance policy" that this represents has to be taken out several times during periods of prolonged uncertainty in foreign-exchange markets. But here the institutional character of large companies becomes a factor. For the responsible treasurer has to cover himself again and again, even though the cumulative cost may be excessive, because he dare not take the risk of being caught uncovered at the moment of the devaluation. Many companies had their sterling book well covered on 19 November 1967, Devaluation Day. Singer made a small profit. The Firestone Rubber Company broke roughly even. International Harvester, Texas Instruments and IBM were also covered. The Xerox Corporation was so well placed that it made a windfall profit of over $4 million.

Here is a clear instance of conflict between the commercial interests of the international group and those of particular national authorities. Responsibility to their international shareholders requires these companies to protect their own interests and to do what they can to circumvent the intention of national exchange-control regulations. During the intermittent storms in the foreign-exchange markets between 1967 and 1969, sterling continually came under pressure in the early afternoon. It was clear that this was the result, allowing for the trans-Atlantic time difference, of financial controllers in the United States reaching their exchange-market judgement for the day and giving their selling instructions to their British and other European subsidiaries.

The transfer-pricing problem

Cumulatively, it was the increasing monetary freedom of the international company and bank that broke the world's monetary system in 1971. And the behaviour of giant corporations in moments of international monetary crisis, brings out one potential conflict with national interests. But, in a more pervasive and permanent style, through their operations international groups have in their hands the power to turn the aims of any given national policy.

The most pervasive aspect of this power is transfer pricing, or the way in which a price is settled for sales or other transactions between various parts of the same international group. To the individual company, this is no more than an internal accounting convention. To the national economies, through which these prices pass, this is central to economic policy, taxation and everything else.

An international and integrated company has a flexibility about the way in which it sets its prices that is not possessed by a company operating on a narrower stage. Every product and every market, certainly, has its own peculiarities and limitations. But it is clear that the larger the company, and the more internationally inter-related the processes of manufacture, the easier it is to arrange for profit and loss to be shown at chosen accounting points in the total system, regardless of the true profitability, by adjusting the national internal pricing.

A European executive, who had worked for an American plumbing supplier with European subsidiaries, answered the question of how prices were set. "In my company, for which I managed all European marketing operations, inter-company pricing was concentrated at the European Head Office and was determined in relation to the general strategy of the corporation and to the particular situation of any individual subsidiary, including its competitive position."[16]

This statement about the way in which one major company established its prices, for both internal and external purposes, makes some critical points. First, the individual foreign

138

subsidiary often has little or no freedom of decision over the price at which it buys its components from other parts of its international group, nor over the ultimate selling price of its products. Secondly, pricing is seen primarily as a component in a marketing strategy for a particular place at a particular time. It is not primarily related to production costs, or even short-term maximisation of profit. If the competitive position of the plumbing supplier in one part of Europe is weak, and if lower prices are accordingly considered the proper marketing strategy, then the inter-company pricing will be adjusted to ensure that the final products can be brought to that particular market at a low price. The group's overall profit can be raised by making up profit margins in markets where the competitive position is stronger. For the company, such an overall, co-ordinated marketing strategy is clearly logical. Indeed, to operate in any other way would be to ignore the potential that exists, through the international nature of the corporation. But it means that national interest is correspondingly subordinated to corporate strategy. It means in particular, that, in countries where one or a small number of international companies have established a dominant market position, the consumer will probably have to pay a higher price, because the companies involved have the chance of exploiting their position, in order to recover the cost of their more aggressive selling tactics in places where their market share is less satisfactory.

The capacity to adjust transactions, so that profits and losses are shown wherever it is most convenient for a particular purpose, is virtually boundless for an international company. It starts in small ways. When an executive from the parent company visits a subsidiary, who pays the expenses? When a subsidiary is given financial or managerial advice, does it pay for it; and, if so, how much? Does the subsidiary raise money on the local market for its expansion, or does it retain its earnings and not pay a dividend to the parent company, or does it get an ordinary intra-company loan from the parent company?

One excellent study of this issue found clear evidence that the prices for goods and components, passed between international subsidiaries within one international group, were juggled.[17] The authors were not able to come to any firm conclusion about the extent of such practices. They quoted instances of companies where there had been a full-scale attempt to use such methods, but where the consequent internal book-keeping was so complex that the idea had to be dropped. They quoted, however, the specific example of Swiss-owned subsidiaries in the United Kingdom.[18] Nine such subsidiaries consistently showed a very high proportion of capital debts owing to their parent companies. The average was 23 per cent of the subsidiaries' total capital in 1959, and 37 per cent in 1967. The suggestion was that, from the point of view of overall taxation, Swiss companies preferred to get money out of their British subsidiaries in the form of interest payments on loans, or as royalty payments, rather than in the more usual form of dividends paid out of profits. This consideration would not apply to American-owned subsidiaries in the United Kingdom. For, in American tax law, payments from subsidiaries in any form would be taxed at the full American rate. In the Swiss case, tax is not charged on interest payments; and this form of remittance to Switzerland avoids the British tax on dividends paid out of profits, since interest payments are allowed as an expense against tax. The study suggests that this is, at least, part of the reason why Swiss subsidiaries in the United Kingdom consistently show a lower rate of profit than their American equivalents.

With Swiss-owned pharmaceutical companies in the United Kingdom, for instance, the study showed that, between 1961 and 1965, five Swiss subsidiaries showed an average rate of profitability less than half that of American-owned subsidiaries, and at least 30 per cent lower than similar British, French, German, Dutch and Swedish companies in the United Kingdom. Part of the reason for this was suggested by an official report on the British pharmaceutical industry in 1967:

Foreign firms reported a much higher cost of materials as a percentage of the total cost of manufacture than did British firms. . . . The highest percentage for manufacturing costs is shown by companies owned in Switzerland, but a large part of these costs represents materials at an advanced stage of manufacture, supplied by their parent companies at prices which as previously stated are not on an open market basis.[19]

The 1967 Sainsbury report led to several years of intensive discussion between the British Ministry of Health and drug companies, to examine whether the public interest was being served. The most voluble protest came from foreign-owned drug companies at the way in which pressure was put on their pricing structure.

One outcome was that in September 1971 Roche, the British subsidiary of the Swiss Hoffman – La Roche group, was referred to the Monopolies Commission over the supply of two branded tranquilisers, Librium and Valium, to the National Health Service. The *prima facie* case was that, while the manufacturing, packaging and selling costs, for example, of Librium, were £1·70 for 1,000 tablets, the retail price was £10. The case also raised directly the question of the Swiss company's transfer-pricing policy. For it exported the drugs in bulk to the United Kingdom, where the only further processing required was to make up tablets and capsules.

Swiss parent companies in these circumstances have been reluctant to make known the basis of their intra-company accounting to the British authorities. And the potential for adjusting downwards the true profit coming to the British sub-sidiary from this drug business is considerable. The British authorities were clearly surprised that, with such a high mark-up in the retail price and with relatively low production costs, the British subsidiary should have shown such restrained profits. National authorities have throughout experienced difficulty in getting accounting information from Swiss parent companies, over whom they have no legal powers. The Swiss companies themselves have argued that the British were asking for account-ing information that was not even required by their own national authorities.

Similar considerations certainly apply to the international oil companies, which, in most cases, operate European subsidiaries at little or no profit, and therefore pay little or no company tax in those countries. BP, for example, pays no direct taxation at all in the United Kingdom. The various tax authorities know that the oil companies arrange their internal financing so as to balance out the high tax and royalty payments that they make to governments in the oil-producing areas. The German authorities, for example, know that they are not getting a tax yield that is in any way proportionate to the amount of true profit that the foreign oil companies make in the country. They equally know that, if the German taxation rules were deliberately made tougher so as to increase the local tax liability of the companies, these would adjust their internal financing, by raising the cost at which they supplied crude oil and other products to their German subsidiaries.

Oil is, as always, still something of a special case. But similar considerations apply to other big international companies. They apply even in companies like IBM and Philips, which are publicly committed to conducting their intra-company transactions on an objective basis. IBM, for example, charges transactions between subsidiaries on a "cost plus" formula. But why should that be the logical formula? What is "cost" in particular cases? On what basis should the total overhead costs of running IBM be charged to this or that particular component or service?

The suggestion was made, for example, in a House of Commons Select Committee hearing,* that IBM was able to quote a highly competitive price for a computer installation, ordered by the British meteorology service, so as to establish a foothold in a market where previously IBM had little or no position. The IBM tender was, in fact, some 26 per cent lower than the nearest rival offer, thus just getting past the unofficial 25 per cent advantage rule that the British government was then applying in favour of British computer manufacturers. IBM denied that there was any element of "loss leading" on this particular tender price; claiming that it had won the contract on the merits of a straight tender. Nevertheless an international company of that size and flexibility has considerable room for manoeuvre,

* See page 101.

when it wants to set particular prices for particular tactical reasons.

Philips, on the other hand, uses the concept of the "market price" for its intra-group transactions, the "arms-length" price that the subsidiary would, in theory, pay for the component or service, if it were bought outside the company. The concept is completely logical and fair, but its detailed application is less clear. For, in the real world of modern marketing, with special discounts, bulk discounts and a host of other particular pricing arrangements, the market price for an item is a highly flexible concept. It would be perfectly possible for two companies, each using some "arms-length" formula, to import a virtually identical component into the same country at substantially different prices. And with sophisticated components, covered perhaps by patents, there may be no open market against which the correct "arms-length" price could be checked. Quite apart from any deliberate loading of prices in a particular direction, therefore, there exists a large degree of discretion in setting the prices that are charged in intra-company transfers. Yet it is these prices that go into the national accounts, that affect the amount earned or spent in the national balance of payments through exports and imports.

This power to adapt prices to market conditions is the basis of fears about allowing any one international company to dominate a particular industry. At the end of 1970, before the bankruptcy of Rolls-Royce, one Labour Member of Parliament put thus the case for continuing public subsidy to the company: "From our experience of paying extra-high prices for American spare parts for almost every aircraft since the Dakota, we should beware of the balance of payments effects of allowing an American monopoly in the aero-engine field."[20] A senior executive of an international engineering company, referring to a contract which his group had won in a particular country, admitted that the tender price had been unrealistically low. "But," he added, "do they pay through the nose now for spare parts whenever anything goes wrong!"[21]

It is for such reasons that there is widespread public disquiet about the near-monopoly position that IBM enjoys in computers over so much of the industrial world. Only in the United Kingdom is there a non-American company with anything like a healthy share of the market. IBM is thankful, in fact, for the continued existence of this British company, International Computers Ltd. It provides them with evidence, for European opinion and for the American anti-trust authorities, that IBM faces real competition, while at the same time the competition is not, in truth, excessive.

Canada is the most extreme example of an industrial country where the production plans, pricing policy and capital movements of American corporations have largely made the local economy and monetary system an extension of the American. It was recognition of this fact that led the Canadian government to float the exchange rate for the Canadian against the United States dollar in 1970. Its balance of payments and banking system are so dominated by the movements of long-term investment funds and short-term capital to and from the United States that it is difficult, if not impossible, to talk sensibly about whether, and by how much, the Canadian dollar is overvalued or undervalued. The decision was therefore taken to let the rate float.*

It was the first breach in the wall of fixed exchange rates, which finally collapsed in 1971. It was a decision that offended the International Monetary Fund at Washington. For the guardians of the world monetary system have worked on the assumption of independent national currencies, reflecting the independent sovereign states that are its members. In that situation, individual currencies remained fixed in relation to each other, except for periodic revaluations and devaluations when the strains become excessive. The Canadian decision, however, was an admission that international industry and

* The Canadian dollar had already experienced one prolonged period of floating in the foreign-exchange markets from 1951 to 1962. But in the 1950s the whole of the industrial world was only moving by steps away from war-time controls and direction, towards free convertibility of national currencies on the basis of fixed exchange rates. Canada's action in 1970, however, was a complete reversal of the post-war trend, which Canada itself had finally accepted in :962.

banking had over-ridden the political distinction between Canada and the United States. It was in recognition of this fact, indeed, that Canada was exempted from the terms of the United States Interest Equalization Tax in 1964 – the tax designed to protect the American reserves by making it unattractive for foreigners and foreign companies to borrow money in New York. Canada was, similarly, exempted from the 1965 voluntary foreign-credit restraint programme for American corporations operating abroad, and from President Johnson's mandatory control programme in 1968. Consequently, borrowing in the United States on behalf of companies and subsidiaries in Canada rose steadily during the 1960s, to pass $1,700 million during 1969 alone.

The Canadian example is exceptional, at least among developed countries. But the dependence of some newly sovereign countries (for example, Botswana and Lesotho on the Republic of South Africa, or the Niger Republic on France) is even more total for the same reason. And the Canadian experience is, to varying degrees, shared by all other industrial countries as well, with the measure reflecting the extent that their industry is international. The process has undermined many of the traditional instruments of national economic policy.

Tariffs undermined

The first of these is the power of national trade tariffs. Whether their retention is seen as an acceptable means of protecting a domestic industry, or whether their removal is seen as a way of encouraging more rational trade and production patterns, the international corporation now has certain powers to nullify. Historically, the main motive for foreign direct investment before the Second World War was the desire to get into markets sheltered behind high protective walls. That power still obtains, even though the main motive for recent international integration has been less negative. International industry, however, having established its supply patterns and its market shares, will not lightly or rapidly change them, just because governments

145

have made some marginal adjustment to import tariffs. Almost the only observed change in production patterns, for example, in response to the steady abolition of all tariffs within the European Free Trade Area has been a degree of extra specialisation in Austria on certain types of tyre production and the transfer of the Swedish garment industry to Portugal.* For the bulk of industry, particularly in the more sophisticated areas, the level of tariffs is no longer more than a marginal consideration. If all the tariffs in the industrial world were abolished by the stroke of a pen tomorrow, the change in the pattern of production over the following ten years would be surprisingly slight. It was remarkably slight in the European Economic Community in the first phase of its existence.

It is inevitably so. For the major industrial sectors, like oil, chemicals, motor cars, motor-car tyres, computers and electronics, have marketing, production and other interests that are substantially more important than a few percentage points on a typical industrial tariff. There have always been tacit market-sharing agreements, where, as a result, tariff changes or other similar acts of government policy are unlikely to affect trade patterns as much as might be expected. But now these arrangements, proscribed or at least not encouraged by national law, are becoming an increasing and built-in part of single, international groups. These corporations establish their internal market-sharing arrangements, for the sake of efficiency and profit, arrangements that cannot be rapidly adjusted to tariff changes.

This aspect has far-reaching consequences for national government policy, towards monopolies and trusts. These consequences are examined in the final chapter. But to take one example here, Dunlop and Pirelli engaged in close international

* Swedish textile companies have largely disappeared during the 1960s, with Swedish demand being met from imports, because the difference in wage costs between Sweden and Portugal is so marked that, in a labour-intensive industry, competitive prices could not be maintained in Sweden. This parallels the way in which the textile industry in the United States has moved from the high-wage, unionised north-east to the low-wage south. The key, however, is that some factor as marked as the wage differential between Sweden and Portugal is required before there is any rapid and significant change as a result of tariff changes.

co-operation for many years, before their final merger in 1971. Dunlop sold its plant in Brazil to Pirelli, for example, since it was jointly felt that Pirelli could make better use of it. Together with the largest German tyre maker, Continental, both companies had a joint venture in Germany for the manufacture of steel cords, used in making the heavy "radial ply" tyres for trucks. Pirelli made Dunlop tyres in Italy, and Dunlop made Pirelli tyres in France. No change in tariffs is going to upset that sort of market-sharing arrangement between two such companies easily. Within one single international group, rapid change is even less likely.

The same considerations apply to other national policy weapons. At the end of 1968 the German government introduced what was in effect a tax on exports in a vain attempt to reduce the German balance-of-payments surplus and thus reduce the pressure on it to revalue the German mark.* At the same time the British government introduced an import-deposit scheme to hold down the level of imports into the United Kingdom.† Neither measure had much effect on trade, though categoric proof, in the nature of the comparisons, is impossible. The major German companies (either as international corporations in their own right, like the chemical giants, or as partners in international joint ventures and other marketing or production arrangements, like the steel companies) could not make significant trading changes in response to some marginal and temporary change in Value Added Tax rates. The same applies to the 25 per cent or so of British trade that is, in effect, the movement of components within single industrial groups.

This company independence applies increasingly to devaluation (or revaluation) of a currency itself, the ultimate weapon in national economic policy. After the November 1967 devaluation of sterling, there was a period of two years during which official opinion was openly surprised at the way in which exports and imports did not react to the changed terms of trade. Part

---

* The mechanism was a reduction in the rebate on the Value Added Tax, normally made on exported goods.

† Initially, a six-month forced loan to the government of half the value of certain imports.

of the answer was unwise domestic economic policy in the period immediately after devaluation.* But a large part was due to the integration of international industry. Even a $16\frac{2}{3}$ per cent devaluation could make no difference in the short-term to an international production process. Take a group like Philips, operating on a European scale, with a component supply network spread even more widely about the world. Imports of Philips components to subsidiary British factories had to continue and simply cost more in foreign exchange. There was no way in which the British market could rapidly be supplied with "British" Philips refrigerators, in response to the changed terms of trade. For the company's European refrigerator-making capacity was already concentrated in Italy. There was no way in which "British" Philips could take advantage of the changed terms to export small tape-recorders. For Philips' production of this item is concentrated in Austria.

The result, in this case, was that the British balance of payments suffered. At the new rate of exchange washing machines shipped to the Philips world-wide marketing network as "British" exports earned less; while at the same time consumer durable goods and the components brought in by Philips cost more. Philips is only taken here as a symbol for international industry. As the process of rationalised integration continues, the impact of devaluation as an instrument of independent national economic policy will be increasingly weakened by these industrial and marketing arrangements. Philips happens to be a Dutch-controlled group, but the argument applies equally to the activities of a British company, operating on the same scale and with the same degree of international integration. The paradox that international industry is free as never before to shift location each time it makes a *new* investment decision, but increasingly inflexible in terms of short-term response to changed conditions, is the double shift in the altered balance of power in favour of the corporation and against national governments.

* It was not, for example, until the spring of 1968 that Roy Jenkins, the new Chancellor of the Exchequer, took steps to rein back home demand to make room for higher exports.

6

Inadequate Countervailing Power

"Rationalisation: The application of scientific organisation to industry, by the unification of the processes of production and distribution with the object of approximating supply and demand."

NUTTALLS' STANDARD DICTIONARY (1929)

This definition of the word rationalisation, the first in the context of industry, was supplied by Sir Alfred Mond of Brunner, Mond, the chemical company that was one of the original constituents of today's Imperial Chemical Industries. It contains within it the nub of the conflict between modern industrial organisation and traditional economic theory. For the underlying philosophy of capitalism (free competition and the operation of market forces) is based on the idea of a constant flux; where efficient use of resources and the optimum level of prices come from the constant conflict between supply and demand. In an industry where demand is greater than supply, prices should rise: and the companies involved should expand or multiply in number. Where demand is lower than supply, companies should contract or go out of business, and prices should fall, with the labour and other resources thus released being put to more popular and profitable employment.

The cartel urge

Such ideal conditions have never existed. And the history of industrial strategy is a constant battle by managements to ensure that they never do. This is the irresistible attraction of cartels and other marketing or price-fixing agreements or understandings, particularly for concerns of any size. In the past twenty years or so, the pressures for "rationalisation" have become progressively more acute, above all in those industries where the cost of the capital plant and equipment requires full, or almost full, use of potential capacity for operations to be economic. In this, the large international industrial corporation has now a historically unique capacity to rationalise. It was the search for such "rationalisation" that created the great cartels and trusts of the past. But the group of really giant international corporations is in a much stronger position than a traditional cartel. For the experience of cartels, however formal, is that in the end they always begin to disintegrate. There is always someone who thinks that he can do better by breaking out of the club.

The case of the Swiss watch industry is a recent example of the way in which cartel agreements come under centrifugal pressure. During the 1930s, in order to protect the interests of the Swiss watch industry, a powerful trading group, known as "The Club", was formed. Its purpose was two-fold. It was designed to ensure the continuing quality of Swiss watches; and it worked to preserve profit margins on their manufacture. The Club established rules whereby the participating ninety manufacturers sold only to participating retailers (some nine hundred by 1970), who in turn handled no other makes of watches in their shops. The discipline of The Club was maintained with fines and expulsion. Omega-Tissot accounted for about half The Club's watches in 1970; Zenith, Certina, Longines and Eterna together produced another quarter of the total. In 1970, frustrated by the limitation placed on it to sell through these nine hundred jewelry shops, Fortis cut its prices and decided to sell through department stores. The calculated risk appears to have been justified. Other members of The Club were then drawn into the mass market at lower prices. Fortis, with an annual production of just under 1 million watches (out of a total Swiss production of some 150 million watches and clocks each year), was one of the smaller manufacturers in The Club. Under aggressive management, it saw better possibilities from independent operation than from keeping the rules of a cartel, where the established jewellers, with shops in tourist haunts and other choice franchises, continued to favour the larger and better-known companies. And so it will always be with cartels, though some may have a considerable life, before they fall asunder.*

Oil, as one would expect from the nature of the industry, provided a fertile ground for cartels and restrictive agreements before the Second World War, just as today it provides the basis for some of the most "international" corporations. These inter-war cartels and other restrictive agreements have influenced the shape and traditions of the international oil industry to this day, though in each case the precise arrangements have long since broken down. It was the inter-war period that saw the introduction of the "Gulf-plus" pricing system, the principle that oil was to be sold everywhere in the world at the price at which it was exported from the United States ports in the Gulf of Mexico, *plus* the assumed cost of transport from the Gulf. This was a system that ensured massive profits on any operations where cheaper oil could be produced elsewhere and supplied to customers along shorter transport lines, with lower costs than would have been involved in shipping it from the American Gulf ports. The British authorities protested at this pricing system during the Second World War, when the Ministry of War Transport found that oil from the Persian Gulf, being used in the Indian Ocean and the Middle East, was carrying a phantom freight differential, to bring the price up to that for oil that might have come from the Gulf of Mexico.[1] The British government never discovered the full facts, though

---

* In some ways, the archetype for an international cartel was the great munitions trust, established in 1897 and including Krupp, Vickers, Armstrong, Schneider, Carnegie and Bethlehem Steel. Between the wars, there was the powerful electrical cartel, with General Electric of America at the hub; and links with the Compagnie des Lampes in France, Osram in Germany, Philips in the Netherlands, AEI and GEC in Britain, and other companies in Japan, China and Hungary.

the oil companies agreed to establish an additional "basing point" in the Middle East for purposes of calculating costs.

Even so, the oil companies were able to operate on staggering profit margins. By early 1948 Persian Gulf crude oil was selling at $2·22 a barrel, the high point. Exposure, partly by Paul Hoffman, head of the European Co-operation Administration, which was running the Marshall Aid Plan in Europe, brought the price down to $1·75 a barrel. Even with this reduction, the American oil companies admitted that they were making profits of 91 cents a barrel in 1948, and 85 cents in 1950. It is against that historical background that militant governments in producing countries have come to believe that the oil companies can always afford to pay more in royalties and tax. Even with much slimmer profit margins today, the oil companies still make their main profits out of supplying crude oil to refineries, and not from refining or selling petroleum products.

Tugendhat's sympathetic study of the growth of the international oil industry is replete with phrases that, sometimes unconsciously, illustrate the way in which those involved were determined to contradict the basic tenets of the open-market economy. Henri Deterding of Shell, Walter Teagle from Standard Oil of New Jersey, and Sir John Cadman, head of Anglo-Persian, were working constantly "to curtail excess production", particularly from the newly exploited Arabian peninsula. The high point of this close co-operation was the so-called Achnacarry Agreement in 1928.

In an effort to stem the rising tide of competition the big three agreed to try to freeze the market in its existing mould. They were to combine their interests and share each other's facilities – refineries, storage, tankers, and the rest – in order to present a united front against companies trying to break into new markets, price cutters, and other disturbing elements. In this way they hoped to derive the maximum benefit from their control of the new oilfields in Iraq and Venezuela and of their other fields spread across the world; each field would supply the markets nearest to it, thereby saving the cost of unnecessarily long tanker voyages.[2]

Even the oil companies found it difficult wholly to prevent

"competition breaking out" between the wars. In the post-war period, though under much greater pressure from governments in producer countries and under more detailed scrutiny from their own national authorities, the major oil companies have operated as a restrained oligarchy. The oil companies have, in fact, signposted the way along which all high-capital industry is progressively going. The present position on that road differs for each particular industry: sometimes for historical and political reasons, more often because of technology and marketing. Formal cartels have been difficult to maintain and yet more difficult to establish since the war, largely as a result of the vigilance of the American anti-trust authorities, operating both within and without the geographical limits of the United States. But the more capital-intensive the industry, the more that market control determines whether profit can be made, the more an industry has been concentrated, first, in the hands of an international oligopoly and, then, increasingly in the growing power of one or two giant international corporations.

In this sense, a particular international corporation like IBM has become a cartel within itself. Market sharing and pricing arrangements are no longer the difficult and unstable preserve of traditional cartels, subject to constant harrassment by anti-trust officials, such as those from the United States Department of Justice. They have become matter for management decision. This is not to say that the decisions are simple, or that the results may not often be to the advantage of some consumers, or that there are not tensions and arguments within an international corporation, which may at times be akin to those between separate companies. It is simply that these conflicts are resolved within one organisation and the decisions taken by one responsible management, increasingly at head office. The forecasting of demand, the provision of capacity to supply that demand, the countries in which production should be carried out, the elimination of "wasteful" competition; all these are the imperatives of large-scale modern industry. Increased market power makes this managerial task easier; and, therefore, it is increased market power that such companies seek.

153

This is the revolutionary change in the position and flexibility of international management which has made an anachronism of so much of political economy. The revolution has now upset the traditional tripartite balance: between the managers, representing their own interests and those of their shareholders; the trade unions, representing the sometimes conflicting interests of their members and of themselves as institutions; and government concerned variously to protect, as part of the "public interest", the supposed interests of the state and to protect the citizen, above all as a consumer. For governments have only just woken to the implications of the change; and organised labour has not in general even reached that point.

Labour's slow reaction

Trade unionists have been particularly slow to appreciate the implications of this new managerial power. In 1970, for example, there was great pleasure at the long-term employment prospects in the British motor-car industry when Ford (UK) was given the task of making engines for the Ford Pinto – the "sub-compact" car with which Ford hoped to make a major impact in the domestic American market. Yet the main reason Ford made that decision was not the excellence of British engineering. It was that, with the average level of wages and salaries lower in Britain* than in the United States, it was thought possible to produce the engines at a significantly lower cost there than in the United States, thus lowering total costs. The announcement was widely and uncritically hailed as the biggest export contract ever achieved by the British motor-car industry. Yet it was a decision that could be reversed without formal reference to government or unions. Thirteen months later Ford announced that all production of Pinto engines in Europe would be phased out by 1973.

In this case Ford had made a miscalculation and decided to cut their losses. But, in principle, the original Pinto decision was identical to the process by which American companies have

* And in Germany where the engines are also made.

154

set up assembly lines in Japan, South Korea, Formosa or Mexico, to produce for the American market. In the past twenty-five years, American-based companies have set up an estimated eight thousand foreign subsidiaries, mostly in manufacturing industry. The consequent loss of jobs in the United States would have occurred equally if industries had grown up spontaneously (with the advantage of cheap labour) in other countries to produce goods which were then imported into the United States, or sold in third markets. But there is one critical difference, created by the international company. Many of these migrating companies are in industries where the United States has an unassailable lead in technology and research, publicly and privately financed. The productivity of American industry should, therefore, be so much higher, the new processes patented so much more numerous that, despite higher labour costs, United States industry should be able to trade competitively with the rest of the world. Where corporations move proprietary techniques to take advantage of cheap labour, jobs are being exported by managerial decision, motivated by an understandable desire to maximise profits.

One of the more exotic of these migrations has been that of the American frozen-strawberry business to Mexico. American food-processing companies have moved south of the border in search of cheaper labour. The result is that imports of "Mexican" strawberries have substantially killed the Louisiana strawberry industry: these imports were running at 88 million pounds, worth about $15 million, in 1969, depressing related employment in Louisiana, and boosting Mexican foreign-exchange earnings. This is a "normal" example of relatively unsophisticated industry moving to cheap labour.

Of greater significance for the changed balance of power between management and labour is the mobility of more sophisticated industry, either through direct investment or through licensing agreements. Amongst American television-set manufacturers, RCA, Ford-Philco, Zenith and Admiral have all started production for the American market in Formosa; attracted by cheap, disciplined labour and other more direct financial inducements. In 1969, Westinghouse closed a television-manufacturing plant in New Jersey and moved the production to Canada. Westinghouse began to import television sets from Canada, as well as sets made in Japan by other companies, imported and sold under a Westinghouse label. Warwick Electronics have moved production from Arkansas and Illinois to Mexico. By 1970 virtually all radios and tape-recorders sold in the United States were manufactured elsewhere, often by United States companies or under American licences. By then about 50 per cent of black-and-white television sets and about 25 per cent of colour television sets were similarly made abroad. The stage has been reached where a home movie/tape recorder, invented and patented by the Ampex Corporation, will never be made in the United States, because Ampex has preferred to sell the licence to Japanese companies and import, rather than to manufacture itself in the United States.

The General Instrument Corporation has, in this way, become the biggest private employer in Formosa. By 1970 it had some twelve thousand workers on its books, making components previously manufactured and assembled in New England. General Instrument also has production facilities in Portugal, where labour is relatively cheap. In 1970 Motorola shut down a plant making television picture tubes and sold the manufacturing equipment to a Hong Kong subsidiary of the American company, General Telephone and Electronics. The Singer Corporation and Burroughs have both stopped making electronic desk calculators in the United States. Their models are now made under arrangement in Japan, by Hitachi and other companies, and then imported under Japanese labels and marketed by Singer and Burroughs. Two out of every three Singer sewing machines sold in the United States are manufactured abroad. Remington typewriters are now made in Japan and imported. Litton Industries shut down its Royal Typewriter plant in the United States and bought, instead, Imperial Typewriters in Britain and Triumph and Adlerwerke in Germany. The list could be continued all but endlessly.*

* This process of migration has not been confined to American corporations

156

There are two fundamental ways in which the changing pattern affects trade unionists and workers in general. Both relate to the fact that the whole framework of labour relations and wage bargaining in industrial countries is based on the relative positions of management and labour within the limited context of a national economy. This is quite independent of whether any particular negotiations or industrial dispute reaches the stage of a physical strike or lock-out. The relative bargaining strengths of the two sides determine the whole fabric of industrial relations.

This equation is fundamentally altered, first when the production process itself becomes mobile, when management can, credibly, claim the ability to close down jobs in one country and offer them in another. Secondly, it is altered fundamentally when the effective responsibility is removed from the local management, with which the national unions are ostensibly negotiating. These twin processes are well established. Yet, by the end of the 1960s, trade unionists had done little more than hold a scattering of conferences to discuss the implications. The British trade-union movement, in particular, has evinced a myopic insularity.

The changed situation was well illustrated during the major strike suffered by Ford (UK) during the early part of 1971. The decision to resist high-wage demands (in contrast to another American motor-car subsidiary in Britain, Chrysler, which had decided, shortly before, on commercial grounds, to concede substantial wage claims) was taken by Ford of Europe, acting in close liason with the American head office. This decision suited the then policy of the British government, eager to slow the rate of wage inflation, even at the cost of major industrial unrest in the short term; and Henry Ford II had a much publicised lunch with the Prime Minister at No. 10 Downing Street, which underlined this community of interest. Ford took the decision mainly because it was so concerned to stop the erosion of the labour cost advantage that it enjoyed by manufacturing

The British company, Plessey, for example, has set up factories in Portugal, Malta and Barbados for making the ferite cores for computer memory systems.

157

in Europe, and because unlike Chrysler, it was in a position to stand the strain of the strike by switching some production to Ford of Germany at Cologne.

There have been embryo attempts by trade unionists to establish international shop-floor solidarity, in order to provide some countervailing power in tactical situations of this sort. These have not had any general success. With Ford, for example, in this case, the greater part of the Cologne work force consisted of non-unionised migrant labour. By 1970 most of the unskilled workers at Cologne were Turkish. Five years earlier there had been mainly migrant Italian workers, who were slowly becoming unionised and potentially more militant, but these had been replaced when their contracts expired. This is another example of the flexibility possessed by the modern management of an integrated industrial company, against which the present power of the trade unions is insubstantial.

A similar pattern affected negotiations between a subsidiary of the Canadian corporation, International Nickel, at Swansea in Wales, and the British Transport and General Workers Union. A proposed productivity deal included a penal sanction clause, which the union was not prepared to accept. In the middle of these negotiations, the corporation became involved in a domestic strike in Canada. As a result, it suited the company to continue a production shut-down at Swansea. The company sat out a strike at Swansea for four months; whereas its negotiating position would have been significantly weaker if the Canadian extracting plant had been on stream and the Welsh subsidiary needed to play its part in the integrated production process.

The reasons that trade unionists have been unable to produce an effective response are clear enough. They were concisely expressed in a paper prepared for a seminar organised by the British Trades Union Congress in October 1970, the first such discussion organised centrally by the British trade-union movement: "The most fundamental problem of all, however, is the very proper jealousy with which national trade union leaders guard their own sphere of influence and the quite natural reluctance of the average trade union member to become involved in the problems of people beyond his own frontiers." The paper quoted the results of a survey conducted amongst Chrysler's Canadian workers. Asked whether they would support Chrysler workers in the United States, England and Mexico (or take other forms of action, such as working to rule, paying increased union dues, or giving public moral support), 53 per cent said that they would strike in support of Chrysler workers in the United States; but the figures for England and Mexico were 10 per cent and 9 per cent respectively. With an unequivocal statement of the obvious, the TUC paper concluded from this: "The willingness to support American workers in clear. However, the degree of international solidarity with regard to English and Mexican workers is relatively low."

Trade unions experienced other substantial difficulties in formulating their practical policies towards international companies during the 1960s. Because of differing national trade-union structures, it was not always easy to find matching partners in other countries for discussions of mutual problems. This is something that afflicts in particular the British trade-union movement, which is organised not on an industry-by-industry, but on a craft-by-craft basis. Other trade-union movements, notably the German, are based on an industrial structure, with all the workers in a particular industry and company belonging to the same union.*

The split in the world trade-union movement between a Communist and an aggressively non-Communist federation has also inhibited co-ordinated discussion and action. As a residual consequence of the Cold War, trade unions affiliated with the International Congress of Free Trade Unions (ICFTU) have been unable to converse with unions affiliated with the Communist World Federation of Trade Unions (WFTU). This inhibition has been ideologically and practically most strong, in both federations, at the leadership level. It has affected, in particular, the willingness of the American trade unionists to

---

* With the exception, in the German case, of clerical workers, who are represented by a single union in all industries.

take part in joint consultation. In practical terms, the most serious consequence has been that the majority trade union in both France and Italy, the Communist-dominated Confédération Générale du Travail (CGT) and the Confederazione Generale Italiana del Lavoro (CGIL) respectively, have been cut off from the mainstream of international trade unionism.*

Trade unionism on the international level has also to contend with the clear trend during the late 1960s for union power to shift from the titular leadership back to the shop floor. There is a marked trend in Western Europe for rank-and-file trade unionists more and more to ignore the conventional authority of their leadership. This has manifested itself in the steady pressure of unofficial strikes, most noticeably in the United Kingdom, but in other countries as well. The leaders of national trade unions are being pushed by, rather than leading, their members. To some, this process is the regeneration of trade unionism from the grass roots. To others, it is a disturbing injection of indiscipline, even anarchy, within the trade-union movement. On either interpretation, or a combination of them, it is a process that for the moment makes it more difficult for organised labour to formulate a strategy to match the flexible power of international management. For a characteristic of international management is that more and more of the critical decisions are removed from the individual plants and subsidiary companies. In contrast, the principle of this new unionism is that power should return to, and come again from, the workers on the individual shop floor. This contradiction of aims – more localised and effective union democracy on the one hand, and more genuine say in the affairs that determine industrial reality on the other – is one which the trade-union movement has not

* The existence of the European Economic Community has contributed here to the beginnings of a thaw. There are now a number of co-ordinating bodies for trade unions in Brussels, created because of a need for organised labour to have a lobby in the formulation of community policy and the detail of its application. This process is drawing the Communist and non-Communist unions together by stages at a practical level. The CGIL, also for internal political reasons, has come out of its international isolation and the CGT is following it with bureaucratic caution.

yet begun to solve. There is no facile answer. For, just as the democratic practices of the Greek city state could not fit larger political units, so giant (and international) industrial structures are not an easy framework for "grass roots" industrial democracy.

There have been a few notable, though isolated, instances where trade unions have taken effective international action. Most thinking and work in this area so far have been done by the International Trade Secretariats, which are designed to act as clearing houses for national trade-union movements. The most active have been the trade secretariats for the chemical industry and for the metal (engineering) workers, both based in Geneva. For the chemical secretariat the main driving force has come from the character of its Canadian Secretary-General, Charles Levinson. With the metal workers, the pressure has come mainly from the American vehicle-workers union, the United Auto Workers, which has pressed strongly, and with some effect, for standing committees of unionists to deal with the international affairs of the three major international American automobile corporations, General Motors, Ford and Chrysler, over the whole range of their international operations. Even here, however, since the trade secretariats are part of the ICFTU, there is the severe practical limitation that the major French and Italian unions have played no direct part in such activity. In addition, since the AFL-CIO has withdrawn from the ICFTU on the grounds that it was beginning to "go soft on Communism," there could be future complications, even within the metal workers' secretariat.

St Gobain – the first major international strike

The most dramatic single event of international unionism was the co-ordinated strike action against the French glass company, St Gobain, in 1969. The French international corporation was engaged in simultaneous, but separate, union negotiations in four countries. In each case the negotiations were being handled in the normal way, by the local St Gobain subsidiary with the

161

national union concerned. Levinson of the International Chemical and General Workers Federation (ICF) in Geneva, who is an adroit tactician and publicist, saw the opportunity of turning this into an "international" negotiation. The mechanics were simple: the financial cost minimal. Logistics were limited to getting delegates to one meeting at Geneva in late March 1969, maintaining contact subsequently by telephone.

This St Gobain action had interesting features, which illustrate the direction in which labour will have to move, if it is to compete with the flexibility of the international company in the 1970s. In 1969 St Gobain was operating in twelve countries. It employed some seventy thousand workers overall in glass making, the company's primary activity; and another thirty thousand in other industrial processes, mainly chemicals. The Glass Section of the ICF had already held a conference in November 1968 – to discuss trends in the industry – which had identified St Gobain as one of the international companies vulnerable to co-ordinated action.

But St Gobain suddenly became an international issue in a fortuitous way. The catalyst was a take-over bid for St Gobain by a smaller, more aggressive and less "established" French glass-making company, Boussois-Souchon-Neuvesel (BSN). There ensued one of the most bitter take-over battles of recent French history, with the greater part of the French banking establishment closing ranks behind St Gobain to beat off the BSN attack. The defence was, at a cost, successful. In the process many, in France and elsewhere, were made aware of the extent to which these two French-based companies were dependent on their industrial operations outside France itself. In the case of St Gobain, a substantial part of the operations is, indeed, conducted through a Swiss holding company, St Gobain Internationale.

As part of its defence, also, St Gobain was forced to reveal more about its financial position and prospects than it had ever done in the past, so as to discourage shareholders from selling out to BSN. In particular, St Gobain's President, Count Armand de Vogüé, announced that consolidated profits after

162

tax were 35 per cent higher in 1968 than in 1967; that net profit and earnings would double by 1971; that the dividend for 1968 would be raised by 22 per cent, with a bonus issue to shareholders of one for every four held. The fact that financial improvements of this sort could be announced for 1968 merely served to underline to the unions the fact that continental law allows a company to reveal very little of its true financial position. The unions, not surprisingly, concluded that the negotiations both in France, with the parent company, and in other countries, with the subsidiaries, were being conducted on an unrealistic basis, without disclosure of the overall profit position, or of any subsidiary breakdown.

Thus, during the take-over battle the unions were presented with evidence that overall profitability was certainly higher than they had been led to suppose. St Gobain had offered its French workers a 3·5 per cent wage increase, promptly accepted by the CGT, which represented less than 5 per cent of the total French work force in the company. The French union side in the St Gobain action was therefore restricted to the smaller trade-union federation, the Confédération Française Démocratique du Travail.

At the Geneva meeting there were delegates representing St Gobain workers in the four countries where wage negotiations were in progress, France, the United States, Italy and Germany. For the Italians, the take-over issue was of particular importance, because the logic of the BSN bid was based on the possibility of rationalising the operations of both companies in Italy, a step which would almost certainly have resulted in redundancies. Representatives of St Gobain workers in Belgium, Norway, Sweden and Switzerland were also present. The decisions taken at that March meeting are worth spelling out in some detail, for they show the ease with which unions can set up effective international support for co-ordinated national negotiations, if circumstances are right and there is a basic will to co-operate.

In the first place, a standing committee was established in Geneva to co-ordinate information about the four national negotiations. It was agreed that no national contract would be signed without the unions involved in the others being informed. There were mutual promises of moral and financial support for unions that might strike during the negotiations. It was agreed to take the necessary steps to ensure that St Gobain were not able to switch production from one plant to another, so as to avoid the consequences of a strike in any one place. At the same time, a call was made for a ban on overtime working at all St Gobain plants.

In each national case, the bargaining issues were different. In Germany, where the union, IG Chemie-Papier-Keramik, is well organised and strong, St Gobain settled rapidly for an 8 per cent wage increase and for terms governing redundancy pay. Since the question of redundancy is critical in an industry that is rapidly introducing the Pilkington patent method for manu-facturing glass, with all its labour-saving possibilities, redund-ancy terms were made a central part of the American negotia-tions by the United Glass and Ceramic Workers of North America. Indeed the American negotiations raised the most interesting issues of principle, from an international unionist's point of view. For St Gobain's American management based its negotiating position on the subsidiary's poor profit showing in 1967 and 1968. In particular, it refused on these grounds to concede wages increases, which had been negotiated for workers in other American glass-making companies, like Pittsburg Plate Glass and Libbey-Owens-Ford. The union in the United States held out for wage and fringe benefit increases that would effectively have averaged something like 9 per cent a year for each of the three years to be covered by the agreement. The union argued that, whatever the profit position on paper of the American subsidiary, it was the profitability of the concern as a whole that mattered.

Levinson, in addition, questioned the profit figures shown by the American subsidiary. He argued at the time that, as a trading concern, the holding company (St Gobain Internationale at Fribourg in Switzerland) was able to follow a pricing policy which transferred earnings to its tax-exempt international division. One way this could be done, he said, was to bill customers directly from Fribourg. The holding company would then receive payment for sales without any goods actually entering the canton of Fribourg. The selling price could be paid by the customer to St Gobain Internationale, which in turn could pay its American subsidiary for producing and shipping the goods, at a price that was nearer to cost. This intra-company pricing policy would have the effect of showing a lower profit and cash flow in the subsidiary's books; and higher earnings for the holding company. Employees, at least, have no means of checking the validity of *per capita* sales or earnings figures, of the sort that are produced in negotiations by the managements of subsidiary companies.

There have been a handful of other examples of international union action. But there has been little practical achievement by unions at the international level. The only major instance, by 1970, of identical pay and work conditions achieved for workers in different countries was the success of the United Auto Workers in getting parity for Canadian and American employees of the big three American automobile manufacturers. This was, however, a somewhat special case, since the same union has Canadian and American members. Under the strong leadership of Walter Reuther, the UAW refused to accept the argument that costs and living-standards were lower in Canada; and that accordingly wage and benefit scales should be lower there. The breakthrough was the acceptance in 1967 of a contract under which Chrysler agreed to give its American and Canadian workers identical terms by 1970. Continental Can, also, has agreed to the same terms for both its American and its Canadian workers.

There have also been a scattering of other instances of international union action at a less ambitious level. British and Dutch workers for Shell, for example, have established some contacts on an informal basis, as have British and Belgian workers for Ford. Italian unions have taken up with Fiat a victimisation case, involving the Fiat subsidiary in Argentina. In 1968, UAW representatives gave critical evidence during arbitration proceedings, on behalf of Australian employees of the General Motors Australian subsidiary, General Motors Holdens. IG Chemie-Papier-Keramik protested effectively to Hoechst, in Frankfurt, about the refusal of the company's subsidiary to recognise the local union in Turkey. Intercontinental Hotels had to recognise a union in Libera in 1967, because of international pressure. A long and particularly bitter strike, in 1969, against the National Biscuit Company (Nabisco) in the United States, was eventually won because international action made it impossible for the company to switch production. British Leyland unions have protested to the management about a subsidiary's behaviour towards unions in Chile. Workers at May & Baker, the British subsidiary of the French Rhône-Poulenc, won a 16 per cent pay rise in 1970, with the help of union intervention at the company's head office in France.

Towards international bargaining

There is now a growing interchange between European and American unions, through conferences; and with European unionists attending discussions between American parent companies and the United States unions primarily involved. The International Metal Workers Federation (IMF) has set up international councils in the automobile industry, such as those for Ford, General Motors and BLMC and other car groups. The function of these bodies, which meet infrequently, is to provide a forum where the overall industrial policies of the international group can be reviewed and compared by representatives of all the workers involved. In 1966, there were IMF conferences on Westinghouse and General Electric. So far, however, except in the limited United States-Canadian examples, there has been no attempt at uniform bargaining. The process has been one of greater exchange of information and the discussion of principles. And it seems likely, given the insularity of trade union movements everywhere, that this will continue to be the main pattern of negotiations for the foreseeable future.

In Europe there have only been two advances towards more

comprehensive discussion of industrial policy with the head office of an international concern; with Philips in the Netherlands and with Brown, Boveri in Switzerland. But the discussions by union representatives with these companies have still been a long step away from negotiations themselves. They have been limited, with Philips, to somewhat philosophic discussions with Frits Philips himself; covering the concern's production problems, its manpower planning within the EEC, its disclosure of financial information, workers' welfare problems, profit sharing, and the like. The first two such meetings took place in 1967 and 1969. When, after the third meeting in 1970, reports appeared in the press suggesting that the company was on the point of agreeing to enter into negotiations of substance, covering the whole of its operations in Europe, there was a sharp reaction from the management, making it quite clear that these talks were not concerned with the detail or substance of any negotiations as such.

It is the institutional power of international companies, rather than the work conditions of their employees, that ought to be a source of concern to trade unions as organisations. During the 1960s some international company managements, particularly American, showed an insensitivity to local conditions that got them into difficulties. But those lessons have been quickly learned. Many American companies now realise that their best course is to give generous terms, so that their workers do not demand that management should recognise local unions. In this way managements in international corporations hope to retain the operational flexibility that is their great strength.

For management errors in labour relations are less significant for organised labour than the success with which many large international corporations handle their labour relations without the unions. A British trade union survey in 1967 found that there was a tendency for substantial foreign subsidiaries in the United Kingdom, particularly the American-owned among them, to take a more systematically anti-trade-union line on the question of recognition than local companies of a similar size.

Kodak has a consistent international policy of resisting union recognition, in favour of company-sponsored workers' representation committees. There have been recognition disputes in the United Kingdom involving the subsidiaries of Caterpillar Tractor, IBM, Gillette, Heinz, Fairchild Camera and other international companies. There is also a stronger-than-average determination to allow only company-sponsored staff unions in all their subsidiaries by corporations such as Continental Oil, Goodyear, Firestone, Nestlé, and some international airlines.

In July 1970 the ICFTU submitted to a United States Congressional Committee the names of IBM, Kodak, First National City Bank, the United Fruit Company and Firestone as particularly marked examples of American corporations which declined to recognise unions, either in the United States or in foreign countries. These companies have been successful because, in the main, they have offered terms of service as good, or better, than the average in the areas where they operate. IBM, for example, in Scotland, an area of traditional trade-union militancy, was able to offer steady and expanding employment opportunities during 1970 and 1971, a period when the general level of unemployment in Scotland was reaching crisis proportions and almost all other companies were laying off labour. This, rather than bad labour relations, is the threat to the power of the trade unions from well-managed international corporations.

The emergence of the multinational corporation has thus materially affected the balance between management and labour within the traditional context of a national economy. It is an altered balance that will remain until the day when organised labour begins seriously to think, feel and operate on a similar international scale. And that day is still long distant.

Monopolies and Competition

No less sharp has been the changed relationship with governments; above all, in this context, in the matter of monopoly, or cartel, policy and the maintenance of competition. For a start, let us look at "competition" and its role, in theory and in practice, as a pressure for keeping down the level of price inflation.

There is at last, slowly, emerging official recognition that giant international companies, with their greatly increased market power, may be part of the reason for the general process of quickening inflation in the late 1960s. In November 1970 the Organisation for Economic Co-operation and Development at Paris produced a report on the problem of inflation.* In a passage on the reasons why prices were increasing more rapidly, it said, ". . . the competitive pressures which have come from the dismantling of trade barriers may gradually weaken and there is a danger that international mergers and growing financial links between large companies in different countries may lessen competition between foreign and domestic suppliers."

The logic is simple. Competition from different companies, not least competition from foreign imports, has helped to hold down prices. Where the structure of an industry has put the market progressively into fewer hands, that pressure is reduced. And the self-perpetuating quality of inflation is enhanced. The incentive to resist inflation and the sanction against raising prices is weakened when the national or world market is so concentrated.

The OECD report declared:

While the growth of multinational corporations and links across national frontiers has been a major factor promoting rationalisation and higher productivity, it also provides increasing scope for monopolistic and oligopolistic practices.

The report continued:

The inability of governments to act against international restrictive business practices is, with the rapid growth of market power of the multinational corporations, of increasing concern. As recent

* The OECD, with a membership of twenty-two countries in 1971, is the organisation where industrial countries discuss and compare their respective economic policies. It also conducts a wide range of research on economic, industrial and scientific policy. This report was prepared for its Economic Policy Committee.

case examples illustrate, there is an urgent need, in the first place, for machinery and powers to secure adequate international exchange of information and – more difficult but more important – machinery to act at an international level against malpractices.

Already, there have been several cases which bear out this judgement. It is enough here to quote two. The first was the decision by the Commission of the EEC, in 1969, to fine for price-fixing ten of the leading European producers of dyestuffs. The Commissions' case was simple: that the companies had raised their prices for dyestuffs simultaneously by identical amounts on three occasions between 1964 and 1967. This was indeed *prima facie* evidence that price competition in dyestuffs was suspended, because ten international companies together, including Du Pont, ICI, CIBA and Geigy, had established a dominant hold on the market. The fines, however, did nothing to strengthen competition as such in future: for the amounts were trifling and were not combined with any more real sanction.

A second case involved farm machinery on the Canadian market. The finding of the Canadian Royal Commission on Prices of Farm Machinery in 1969 was that international companies were indeed entering into restrictive agreements about the prices at which they would sell to the Canadian market. It concluded, however, that there was nothing that could be done about it, since the decisions and agreements were being reached by the companies outside the jurisdiction of the Canadian government.

The size of many of these great corporations and the network of interlocking relationships between them is, without question, reducing the scope for competition in many areas. In frozen foods, for example, Nestlé now owns the Swedish based international frozen-food company, Findus. Findus has been merged with J. Lyons in the United Kingdom. Elsewhere in Europe, outside Switzerland, Findus' activities have been merged with Unilever's Birds Eye division, so that Nestlé is left with a 25 per cent minority share. This is effective rationalisation by Nestlé and Unilever. Yet inevitably it reduces competition. The United States authorities have proved more sensitive to Nestlé's market power than most European governments. By

1970 the American market accounted for about one-third of total Nestlé business. The centre of Nestlé's American strategy in the early 1960s was its 20 per cent holding in the Libby canning company. The American anti-trust authorities objected to any further increase in Nestlé's control. And, because of this active concern by the United States Justice Department, Libby will always be the least integrated part of the world-wide Nestlé empire.

The world market-share position in another type of consumer goods, washing detergents, is more concentrated than in any other. Two companies, Unilever and Proctor & Gamble, account for something like half the total consumption outside the Communist world. In addition, Colgate has about 10 per cent of the world market and the German Henkel group about 4 per cent; so that, together, these four groups alone account for some 65 per cent of the total market. The reason for this concentration is simply that, ever since Unilever so successfully projected Rinso between the wars, the economics of the soap-detergent business has depended on mass advertising for branded products. The consequence is that the price of detergents on the market includes a heavy element of advertising cost.

Another typical example of the way in which rationalised production reduces the inefficient uncertainties of competition is the International Synthetic Rubber Company in England. With Dunlop at 45 per cent as its main shareholder, the other participants include virtually every company of significance in the international rubber business. Firestone and Goodyear have a 19 per cent holding each, Michelin has a 10 per cent holding, while Avon, Pirelli, Uniroyal and BTR Leyland Industries each has a token stake. There is, therefore, no incentive for any of the participants to compete in the British market.

To date, it is only the American anti-trust authorities that have looked at the question of market power in an international context. In the process, they have severely upset companies and governments in other countries. Even then, they have only looked at the question in terms of the likely, or potential, effect on corporate behaviour within the United States. With that limitation, however, they have cast the net exceedingly wide. The merger between the Swiss chemical companies CIBA and Geigy, in 1970, was held up for a full year, because of discussions with the United States Department of Justice. The Americans were concerned, not about the effect of this concentration of power within Switzerland, or even within Europe. They were concerned at the reduction in potential competitive pressures within the United States, where both companies had extensive and nominally independent subsidiaries. The American authorities also subjected to close scrutiny the plans of BP to enter the American market through arrangements with Atlantic Richfield and Standard Oil of Ohio in 1969 and 1970. In this case also, the concern was that a potential external source of future competition for established companies was being removed.

The legality and propriety of extra-territorial extension of national law by the American authorities has been questioned in other countries; when the consequences have been awkward for non-American corporations. The evidence of the 1960s, however, is that a steady development of such extra-territorial concern, going beyond the legal fictions of the nation state, should be developed rapidly; at least if anti-trust and monopoly policy, pursued in the interests of consumers everywhere, is to have any real meaning. It seems that, on this basis, the pattern of American concern, stretching beyond the boundaries of the United States, should be extended. One possibility is the development of an international code of practice, to which all industrial countries subscribe and in which they merge their sovereignty, in order to provide some cohesive policy that effectively matches the international power of the corporation. National policies to promote competition, such as those pursued by the British Department of Trade and Industry, or even those on a regional scale, conducted by the EEC Commission, are paper tigers in comparison with the truly international scope of industrial operations today.

The requirement is particularly urgent in the case of industrial countries, such as the United Kingdom and the other countries of Europe, because of their size in relation to the new concentrations of industrial power. Certainly as long as countries continue to think fundamentally in terms of national econo-mies, industrial logic must force a trend towards ever reducing competitive pressures. Even in the United States, with its vastly greater resources, there was by 1970 a strong body of opinion that the cost of aviation development had become so great that it made no sense to manufacture even two competing airbuses for the 1970s, the DC10 and the TriStar. Other national aircraft industries have long since reached that stage, or even passed it, to the point where only international joint ventures are con-ceivable.

The process of diminishing competition has advanced for European countries in other high-capital-cost industries; and the process is moving down the industrial scale. Shell, for example, wished to build an oil and chemical expansion com-plex at Carrington in Cheshire to come "on stream" in 1975 and costing at least £125 million. The expansion would double the international group's chemical capacity in the United Kingdom and make a substantial increase in its oil-refining capacity.

The planning for the expansion was made in consultation with Shell's international competitors in the United Kingdom market, ICI and BP. Public knowledge of such co-ordinated discussions between supposedly competing companies led to some critical comment at the end of 1969. To meet this criticism, David (now Sir David) Barran, Chairman of the Shell group, gave a detailed analysis of the way in which the decision had been reached.[3]

Barran vigorously denied that there had been collusion with industrial competitors or with the government, or that the con-sultations had contravened the spirit of the Restrictive Trade Practices Act.

Shell, he said, looked at the whole of the free world as a single economic unit. In deciding whether and in which country a new plant should be built, Shell studied the size of particular markets and the forecasts for their growth, the general economic and political stability, the attitude of the government towards the concept of private industrial investment, and other factors, such as the state of industrial relations in various countries.

In this particular instance, it had been decided that the future growth of demand in the United Kingdom for organic chemicals and plastics was good, though not as strong as in much of continental Europe. Shell wished to hold on to its position as the second biggest supplier of organic chemicals to the British market. This had led to the basic question: whether Shell should plan to meet this forecast requirement with imports into the United Kingdom, or from domestic production.

Shell had finally taken the decision to expand British capacity on the basis of prior consultation with its competitors. There had been, and were, good reasons for such consultation. The first was that the cost of this sort of new plant (and the absolute need not only to have it operating rapidly but to keep it operating at or near capacity) made it vital to ensure that the production plans of the major companies concerned coincided. "It would not have been in anyone's interest (our own, our customers or the United Kingdom economy at large) for all three of us to have started simultaneously to build ethylene crackers costing £50–60 million a piece." There were only a few contractors in the world able to build these highly specialised plants. It was important both for them and for the chemical companies that there should be a reasonable spread and pattern to the workload of plant-building put upon them.

Barran continued: "Yes, indeed, we did talk to our competitors, but not how to carve up the market or set up a cartel. What we talked about was rationalising production of basic chemicals and spreading the work-load."

In this case, a joint Shell-ICI study group had been set up, which had reported in October 1968. It had come to the conclusion that the economic performance of all their respective plants would be improved, if they could make arrangements for the mutual transfer of ethylene between their respective plants by pipeline.

Without question the arrangement would help to improve profitability for all concerned. It was, however, a typical further example of the erosion of pure competition between international groups. It could hardly be otherwise.

The Shell-ICI example is only one instance of the sort of

pressures under which international companies operate and the situations in which they can use their operational flexibility and power to achieve "rational" production and marketing. There will be more and more instances, particularly where the level of capital investment involved is such that it can only be commercially justified in circumstances where the risks of the ordinary market-place have been significantly reduced.

In these circumstances there will have to be created a new conceptual framework of policy for the supervision of the consumer and public interest. The prerequisite is that this new framework should be wider than the single nation state, for the industrial operations with which it will be concerned are already on a so much wider basis. Again, this is an area in which there is no sign of national willingness to make the necessary concessions in the direction of pooling national sovereignty. Yet, in this context, national independence is national impotence. And that fact ought to be faced by the politicians and civil servants concerned.

Conclusion

As with the reaction of the trade-union movement there is little or no sign that national governments are, in practice, prepared to make the leap to internationalism that industrial managements have been regarding as commonplace for one and two decades. It seems for the moment as if industrial management is the only organism which has found the capacity to emerge from the restrictive and increasingly irrelevant chrysalis of the nation state. In due course the pressure will become irresistible for a basic change in the attitudes of governments and trade unions alike. But that moment has not yet come: The slow process of development will occupy the whole of the 1970s. It is the managemen' of international corporations which have led the way. And, when the history of the late twentieth century is written, it will surely be said that it was the operations of industry that did more than anything else to undermine the overwhelming dominance of the nation state over the condition of man for the last three centuries.

175

REFERENCES

1 Sovereignty Undermined

1 *Introduction to the World Economy,* Professor A. J. Brown, Allen and Unwin, London, 1966, p. 110.
2 "Multi-National Companies", *Moorgate and Wall Street Review,* Autumn 1968.
3 *Le Défi Américain,* Editions Denoel, Paris, 1967.
4 Interview in *German International,* November 1970.
5 In his essay "The multi-national corporation" in *Management and Corporation 1985,* ed. N. Anshen and G. L. Back, McGraw-Hill.
6 See for example Richard D. Robinson, *International Management,* Holt, Rinehart and Winston, New York, 1967 and H. V. Perlmutter, L'Entreprise Internationale — trois conceptions, *Revue économique et sociale,* May 1965.

2 An Industrial Revolution

1 A. E. Safarian, *The Performance of Foreign-Owned Firms in Canada,* published by the Canadian-American Committee, 1969, page xviii, and, in general for Canada, the same author's fuller study *Foreign Ownership of Canadian Industry,* McGraw-Hill Company of Canada, Ltd, New York, 1966.
2 See Jacques Gervais, *La France Face aux Investissements Étrangers,* Editions de l'Entreprise Moderne, Paris, 1963.
3 Harr was commenting on the USAIA survey dated 10 November 1970.
4 *Harvard Business Review,* January/February, 1967.
5 For an account of that invasion, see Nicholas Faith, *The Infiltrators,* Hamish Hamilton, London, 1971.
6 Speech to the Institute of Directors in London, 5 November 1970.
7 For example, *Le Monde's* English language Weekly Selection for 1 July 1970.
8 *The Case for Overseas Direct Investment.*

3 Ideology

1 Frederic G. Donner, *The World-wide Industrial Enterprise: its Challenge and Promise,* McGraw-Hill, New York, 1967, page 113.
2 Donner, *op. cit.,* page 3.
3 Speaking to a CIOS Congress in Tokyo, 8 November 1969.
4 J. L. R. Anderson, *East of Suez,* Hodder & Stoughton, London, 1969, page 199.
5 Introduction to Donner, *op. cit.,* page ix.
6 See E. P. Thompson, "The Business University", *New Society,* 9 February 1970.

4 A Matter of Identity

1 See Christopher Tugendhat, *Oil: The Biggest Business,* Eyre & Spottiswoode, London, 1968, page 98.
2 Charles Wilson, *The History of Unilever,* Cassell, London, 1954, Vol. II, page 306.
3 Frederic G. Donner, *The World-wide Industrial Enterprise: its Challenge and Promise,* McGraw-Hill, New York, 1967, page 105.
4 Joint article "Developing the International Executive", *European Business,* January 1970.
5 *Sunday Times,* 11 October 1970.

6 Private correspondence.
7 Allan W. Johnstone, *United States Direct Investment in France: an Investigation of the French Charges,* Massachusetts Institute of Technology, 1965.
8 Johnstone, *op. cit.,* p. 89.

5 The Effects

1 Quoted in Peter Wilsher, *The Pound in Your Pocket,* Cassell, London, 1970, page 85.
2 E. E. Williams, *Made in Germany,* quoted in Wilsher *op. cit.,* pages 85-86.
3 See *New Statesman,* 13 November 1970.
4 Frederic G. Donner, *The World-wide Industrial Enterprise: its Challenge and Promise,* McGraw-Hill, New York, 1967, page 35.
5 Evidence to the House of Commons Select Committee on Science and Technology (Subcommittee D) 25 February 1970.
6 See in particular its Fortieth Annual Report, 8 June 1970, pages 145-63.
7 Televised address to the nation, Sunday, 15 August 1971.
8 Daniel P. Davidson, Vice-President and General Manager, Morgan Guaranty Trust Company at the Institute of Bankers in London, 29 October 1970.
9 *Wall Street Journal,* 20 August 1971.
10 Speaking, in this case, at the annual dinner of the American Chamber of Commerce at Brussels, 20 April 1970.
11 Speech to the United States National Foreign Trade Council, 18 November 1969.
12 HM Treasury Press Release 9 March 1970.
13 HM Treasury, June 1970.
14 *European Business,* Summer 1970.
15 "Managing Risks in Foreign Exchange", *Harvard Business Review,* March–April 1970.
16 Private correspondence.
17 Michael A. Brooke and H. Lee Remmers, *The Strategy of Multi-national Enterprise,* Longmans, London 1970.
18 Brooke and Remmers, *op. cit.,* page 223.
19 The Sainsbury Report. HM Stationery Office (Cmnd 3410), London, 1967.
20 Tam Dalyall in the *New Statesman,* 20 November 1970.
21 Private correspondence.

6 Inadequate Countervailing Power

1 See Christopher Tugendhat, *Oil, the Biggest Business,* Eyre & Spottiswoode, London, 1968, page 123.
2 Tugendhat, *op. cit.,* page 101.
3 Talk entitled "The Anatomy of Decision" to the Economic Research Council in London, 25 February 1970.

Index

INDEX

Firestone, 14n, 45, 137, 168, 171; in Belgium, 54; in Liberia, 59
First National Bank of Chicago, 119
First National City Bank, New York, 70, 168
Fokker, 39n
food industry, 47
Ford, 15, 21, 30, 48, 63, 166; in Britain, 22, 84, 94n, 113n, 132, 154, 157–8; in France, 106–7; in Japan, 27; size of, 27, 45
Ford, Henry, 15, 74
Ford, Henry II, 94n, 157n
Ford-Philco, 155
Formosa, 112, 155, 156
Fortes, 68
Fortis watches, 120–1
France: Commissariat du Plan in, 97; foreign investment in, 25, 27–8, 54, 83–5, 97–9, 106–7; mass marketing of food-stuffs in, 47; research and development expenditure in, 33; trade unions in, 160, 163
free-enterprise system, ideology of, 17, 32, 56–7
French language, 70–1

Gaulle, General de, 61, 71, 98; and international corporations in France, 18, 83, 94–5
GEC-AEI-English Electric group, 29n, 99n
Geigy, 170; merger of CIBA and, 15n, 44, 172
General Agreement on Tariffs and Trade (GATT), 92n
General Dynamics, 34n, 36
General Electric, 28, 34n, 43, 70, 75–6, 151n; in France, 99; licensing by, 111, 112; size of, 45; trade unions and, 166
General Instrument Corporation, 156
General Motors, 21, 48, 61, 77, 78; in Argentina, 52–3, Belgium, 132, Britain, 22, France, 30, 98, Germany, 22, 54, Japan, 27, and South Africa, 100; price fixing by, 17; remittance of overseas profits by, 131; size of, 6, 45; trade unions and, 166; USA Department of Defence and, 35; USA executives in subsidiaries of, 80–1; value of overseas assets of, 97

General Motors Holdens, 80, 81, 94n; trade unions and, 165–6
General Telephone and Electronics, 156
General Tire and Rubber, 45
Germany, West, 40, 89, 110; banks in, 118; foreign investment in, 21, 24, 25, 27, 54, 113n; foreign workers in, 89; oil companies in, 127, 128; research and development expenditure in, 33; trade unions in, 159
Gillette, 9, 166
Giscard d'Estaing, Valéry, French Finance Minister, 98, 120
glass industry, 162, 164
Goodyear, 9, 14n, 45, 166, 171; in Luxembourg, 52
Goodyear International Technical Centre, 52
governments: attitude of, to international corporations, 2, 12–13, 18, 38–9, 49–50; balance of power between corporation and, 10–11, 148, 154; subsidies to industry from, 32–6
Greece, 25n
gross national product, 61
Gulf Oil, 45n, 112
"Gulf-plus" pricing system for oil, 151

Harr, Karl G., of US Aerospace Industries Association, 35
Harvard Business School, 72
Heath, Edward, British Prime Minister, 71n
Hegland, David, of General Motors, 80–1
Heinz, H. J., 9, 97, 166
Henkel group (detergents), 171
Herbert, Alfred (machine tools), 63
Hilton International, 68, 69
Hirons, William B., of Du Pont, 81
Hitachi, 156
Hoechst, 15n, 44, 53, 166
Hoffman, Paul, of European Co-operation Administration, 152
Hoffmann-La Roche, 15n, 141
holding companies, 134–5, 162
Honeywell, 53, 99
Hong Kong, 112, 156
Hong Kong and Shanghai Bank, 119
Hoover, 21, 136
hotel industry, 66, 67–9